LIVING BY
GRACE

DAVID R. ANDERSON, Ph.D.
CHARLES C. BING, Ph.D.
FRED CHAY, Ph.D.
PHILIP F. CONGDON, Th.M.
MARK HAYWOOD, D.Min.
MARK RAE, M.Div.

GRACE
THEOLOGY PRESS

Living By Grace

Published by Grace Theology Press

ISBN 978-1-7336223-5-6 (paperback)
ISBN 978-1-7336223-7-0 (ebook)

Printed in the United States of America

First Edition 2021

Contents

Introduction

Dr. Fred Chay

"Grace: you don't deserve it, you can't buy it,
you can't live without it."

RT Kendall

G race is a Rorschach word. Define it and you immediately say a great deal about yourself. Grace is not simply what we say at the beginning of a meal, nor is it simply an esoteric theological term. Grace describes the heartbeat of God toward His people and should describe the heartbeat of His people toward Him.

Grace is not only an essential part of the academic curriculum in seminary or Bible College, but it is also crucial in ministry, in the home, in the workplace, the public square, and in every facet of your life and every relationship you enjoy. Simply put—grace is essential, indispensable, and crucial in all of life. Grace is not only an attribute of God. It is an aspect that should permeate our lives.

Living by Grace attempts to make the case for grace in every corner of our lives. It makes sense that since we were saved by grace, we should live by grace. Since God is grace, we should not only experience His grace but also live within it and give it to others. There have been many sermons and songs, books, and biographies about grace. And that is because grace is at the heart of God and central to the Bible. Grace is at the center of the life of Abraham, Moses, and David as well as the apostles Paul and Peter. Jesus was the perfect personification of grace in all of life. The grace of God and the God of grace is fundamental and foundational to all biblical revelation and the story of the Bible.

The grace of God completely covers and cancels my failure and my sin. It is a free gift, a gift that justifies me forever. It is a gift of love that I could never earn, and it is a gift that I can never lose. Grace tells me that I am totally acceptable before God forever. But grace also shows me how to live today in light of tomorrow. It describes how I do ministry, how I live with family, how I relate with others at work, and in the marketplace.

I invite you to invest some time in the following pages and discover how the grace of God can and should permeate our lives at all levels in all relationships. Our guides are seasoned pastors, theologians, missionaries, and ministry leaders who are well-trained in the scriptures and well-experienced in life. Our approach is not a lecture for the classroom, but lessons from the Scripture to the heart. Our hope is that your heart will be overwhelmed by the goodness of God and His grace to you. Our desire is that you will be more equipped and encouraged to manifest the grace of God in your life.

Chapter 1

Introduction to Free Grace Theology

Dr. David Anderson

When I was in seminary long, long ago in a galaxy far, far away, "free grace" (afterwards FG) was not a phrase we heard much about. It first came to my attention in the '90s. Initially, it came into use to describe an approach to the gospel that opposed what has come to be known as "lordship salvation." John MacArthur came out with his book *The Gospel According to Jesus* in support of the lordship position. Zondervan had published his book but did not want to identify with that position alone, so they asked Zane Hodges, who taught in the Greek department for Dallas Theological Seminary (afterwards DTS) for over twenty years, to write a rejoinder to MacArthur. He wrote *Absolutely Free*. MacArthur's book defended a view that one must surrender completely to the lordship of Christ by committing one's will to obey every command of Jesus in order to go to heaven. Hodges defended the view (indicated by the title of his book) that getting to heaven was a free gift from God to us. The only requirement for receiving this gift was our faith in God's offer.

Though the debate is much more nuanced than just determining the requirement(s) for entering heaven, that question alone, first voiced by the Philippian jailer to Paul ("What must I do to be saved?"—Acts 16:30-31), has preoccupied church history for centuries. One's answer has a profound effect on people in the pew. I once went with an elder in my church to interview a woman for church membership. She began asking us questions like the one above. When we explained that simple trust in the person and work of Jesus Christ was the only requirement, she teared up. I assumed I had offended her somehow, so I asked, "What is it? Something I said?" She replied, "No. I mean yes. I have never heard about this kind of love." I asked her about her church background. She said she came from California and had been a member of a famous pastor's church for fifteen years. "One day I went to church and the pastor said, 'If any of you have an ongoing sin you have wrestled with for many years, then you probably are not a Christian.'" At this point she was quite emotional and said, "I have wrestled with smoking most of my adult life. I think it is a sin because I am destroying my body, but I can't seem to quit. Because of what the pastor said, I have been living in fear that I will not go to heaven when I die."

It reminds me of a conversation I had with Tony Evans, a famous American preacher, while driving to the airport. He asked me, "Do you ever wrestle with pride?" My reply: "Only every day." He responded, "I have wrestled with pride all my life. Does that mean I am not a Christian?" Ongoing sin battles have caused many professing Christians to doubt their salvation. Tony was not doubting his salvation. He was pointing out the problem of anyone thinking he does not have ongoing sin in his life along with believing that ongoing sin is a sign he is not born-again.

The problem of assurance has mushroomed since MacArthur came out with his book on salvation. Not that he alone is the cause. Some of the most gifted and popular preachers in America (John Piper, Timothy Keller, the late R. C. Sproul, Matt Chandler, the late James M. Boice) teach that a person professing to be a Christian who "continues in sin" is not a Christian at all (1 Jn 3:9). Do you continue in sin? How are you doing with that pride problem?

FG theology explains the conundrum of being justified in heavenly places while simultaneously being a sinful person on earth (*simul iustus et peccator*—Martin Luther). FG theology makes a distinction between your inalterable Position *in Christ* and your still sinful Condition *on earth*. The first, our sinless Position in Christ, is established through our justification, while the second, our sinful Condition on earth, is changed for the better through our sanctification. But only FG theology can explain how these two (justification and sanctification) relate to one another in such a way that the gospel of God is not encumbered with requirements that extend beyond simple faith in Jesus. In this brief introduction to FG theology, we do not intend to tell you what we think is wrong with the many competing theologies out there; no, we want to tell you what is right about FG theology. We want to highlight six aspects of FG theology that bring to the child of God greater assurance, greater intimacy, greater motivation, and greater understanding of God than any other system of theology, at least in our estimation.

FG theology allows us to live a "thank-you" life instead of a "have-to" life.

Larry Moyer of EvanTell Ministries is the first I had heard articulate this contrast. He was simply saying if eternal life is a free gift from God, then it should be obvious that we don't "have to be good" to go to heaven. As far as we can tell, all other theologies say we have to be good to get into the pearly gates. Roman Catholicism says we must continue to be good in order to have Christ's character formed in us to the extent we are acceptable to God and get a pass into heaven. That is their view of justification: ongoing infusions of Christ's character throughout our lives, starting with infant baptism, until we make the grade required to get into heaven. If we fall short, there is still the option of purgatory where the purification process (purging) continues until we pass muster. Bottom line: we have to be good in order to go to heaven.

But surely the Protestant Reformation changed all that . . . or did it? The twin towers of the Reformation were Martin Luther and John Calvin, both avid students of Augustine (d. 430 A.D.). Augustine said a professing Christian must persevere in faithful obedience to Christ until the end of his life or he will not be able to go to heaven. This became the fifth point of Dortian Calvinism, called perseverance of the saints. Both Luther and Calvin perpetuated this doctrine. Hence, even to this day, all the denominations spun off from Calvin and Luther believe a Christian has to be good until the end of his life to have eternal life. Jacob Arminius himself was initially a Calvinist, but later generations with leading lights like John Wesley fostered a branch of Christianity known as the Arminians. They, like the Lutherans, taught that Christians must be good until the end of their lives or they lose their salvation. So, the Calvinists said we have to be good, or we never were true Christians to begin with, and the Arminians said we have to be good, or we lose our salvation in the end. In either case, they were teaching a "have-to" life.

Of course, the Calvinists object to being characterized as those who teach a "have-to" life because they claim the necessary good works of the believer are simply external proof of his genuine, internal faith. But this is just double-talk. If something is necessary, then it is a "have-to," a "must," a "requirement." It puts the burden of being good on the shoulders of the professing Christian. Augustine helped mitigate this burden by claiming that God gave a second gift (the first being eternal life) to the professing Christian. That was the gift of perseverance, which God arbitrarily chose to give to some believers and not to others. When asked why God would choose some and not others, Augustine simply explained that it was a great mystery.[1] Mystery or not, the followers of Augustine (Catholics, Calvinists, and Arminians) teach a "have-to be good" life until the end of one's life or heaven's gates are closed.

Of course, this kind of teaching will yield some wonderfully moral people. But what is missing in the lives of so many of them is joy. I spent a summer near Guadalajara, Mexico writing a book. My host was a retired British Petroleum executive from South Africa. He was an Afrikaner raised in the Dutch Reformed faith. He told me no one was allowed to smile while in the church building, especially during services. If one felt a smile coming on, he must retreat from the building and smile outside. Why? Because church is serious business; one's attitude and actions are the difference between heaven and hell. No joy. In fact, Michael Eaton, formerly a Reformed scholar whom we will mention later, wrote his PhD dissertation on why so many of his Reformed friends lacked joy, were legalistic, judgmental, and introspective.[2]

In FG theology we teach a "thank-you" life. We don't "have to" be good to go to heaven. We would always be wondering if we were good enough. But if I volunteer to be good (Rom 12:1-2) because I want to and out of gratitude for what the Savior has done for me, there is joy. A "have-to" life is a job; a "thank-you" life is a joy.

FG theology is the only theology that can give us assurance in this life that we will go to heaven when we die.

I once asked a popular and much published seminary professor if he was one of the elect. He said, "Sure." When I asked him his reason(s) for thinking he was elect, he said because of the good fruit in his life and his continuance in the faith. So, I asked him about Demas, who left Paul and went after this world (2 Tim 4:10). He said, "We don't know the end of the story. He might have come back." But what if he doesn't come back? What would that say about his election? "He wasn't elect." But what if he comes back? What would that prove? "He was elect." But what if he went away, came back, and went away again? What would that prove? "We don't know, because he might come back again?" Well, when are we going to know if he is elect? The answer is obvious: when he dies. This professor looked up from the text and said, "Humph. I guess you can't have assurance in this life."

That's exactly right, if you believe you must endure faithfully until the end of your life in order to be saved. I was talking to another professor at the same seminary and asked him if he thought he was elect. He affirmed that he was. On what basis? "Because I can see the Holy Spirit working in my life through my love for people, my love for Christ, and my love for God's Word." Could you fall? (He has to say yes because of 1 Cor 10:12 that says, "Let him who think he stands take heed unless he falls.") What would that say about your assurance based on your love for people, Christ, and the Bible? He began to squirm and said, "Well, a temporary fall wouldn't prove anything because I could always repent and that would prove I'm elect." "But could you fall and repent and fall again?" He could see where this was going, so he just stood up and said, "Well, I know I am elect," as he walked away.

It is obvious the Catholics can't have assurance of their salvation in this life because they think the question of their justification is not settled until they die. In fact, some of them think the height of hubris is for someone to claim he will go to heaven when he dies. And it is obvious that the Arminians can't have assurance of their salvation until they die because they think they can lose their salvation right up to the point of death because of serious sin in their lives. The only Christians left to ponder the subject are the Calvinists. And they are just followers of Augustine whose misinterpretation of Matthew 24:13 ("He who endures to the end will be saved") made assurance impossible in this life. After all, how will you know if you have persevered until the end?

In fact, in theological circles, students like to debate how many of the "soils" in the Parable of the Sower will go to heaven, assuming the different soils are different people who hear the gospel (the seed that is sown). Some will say all but the first because the person represented by the first soil did not understand the gospel, and the devil took the seed away (Matt 13:19). But the second soil (person) would be saved since the Lukan version of the parable (Luke 8:11-12) says the first "soil" was not saved because he did not believe, implying that being saved was the result of believing. Therefore, the second "soil" might have been saved because he "believed for a little while." If we believe that faith alone is required for eternal life, and justification comes by faith at a moment in time, then the one who believes has eternal life. Luke says the people represented by the first type of soil did not believe, but those of the second type did. For a while. If you are an Arminian, you would conclude that the second type represents those who lost their salvation. Some Calvinists would conclude that the faith of the second type was not saving faith because it was only temporary. If you are truly elect, you will have faith until the end.

So, what do you think Calvin said as to how many of the four were elect? His answer? Potentially none because we don't know if the fourth type of soil kept on producing fruit until the end of his life. Calvin, like his teacher Augustine, thought the non-elect could have fruit that looked like the elect. Only perseverance until the end separated the sheep from the goats.

We like to claim 1 John 5:13 ("These things I have written unto you who believe in the name of the Son of God that you might KNOW that you have eternal life") as proof positive from the promises of God that a new believer can and should have assurance of his salvation the moment he believes. All you have to have for your assurance is that one promise. One promise from God is enough.

"But what about fruit?" someone will ask. Sometimes FG teachers are caricatured as teaching that fruit doesn't matter when it comes to assurance. That's not true at all. Of course, it matters. Every new believer will have some fruit. But that fruit might be internal, as in the fruit of the Spirit. If you have the Spirit, which every new believer does (1 Cor 12:13), then all of His fruit is at your disposal. But how much fruit, how observable is the fruit, what type of fruit—all these questions have subjective answers. So, we claim that the only essential thing we must have for assurance is God's promise(s) in His Word. Spiritual fruit can be corroborating, but not determinative. A "backsliding" Christian might go a long time without much positive, observable fruit. Or false prophets can outwardly display lots of "good fruit" (preaching, giving, worshipping, etc.). **We can see the fruit; only God can see the root.** That's why in the Parable of the Tares, Jesus told his disciples not to try to distinguish between the wheat and the tares; leave that to the Lord of the harvest.

This discussion on fruit segues into another blessing of FG theology.

FG theology delivers us from fruit inspecting.

Well, if I have to keep the faith until the end of my life in order to go to heaven, how will I know that I am faithful enough? And what about my children? How will I know if they are elect or not? And what about my fellow church members? How can I know if they are toeing the line? The answer is obvious: I must inspect my fruit and theirs to determine if I am or they are elect. Interestingly, John Calvin himself said if I look to my own fruit to determine if I am elect, I'm doomed to a life of doubt. We must look to Christ for our assurance. But his successor at the Geneva Academy, Theodore Beza, who taught that God determined who would go to heaven and who would go to hell before He even created anyone, said it doesn't do any good to look to Christ for my assurance since Christ might not have died for me if I am not elect (that He died only for the elect is one of the five points of Calvinism). Hence, the only person I can look at with any certainty is myself, that is, my fruit. The writing of diaries actually began during the Reformation as a way of tracking one's daily sins to help determine if one was one of the elect. Voila! The fruit-inspecting industry mushroomed.

Of course, I can assuage some of my guilt from sins in my life if I notice that my fruit is just a bit better than your fruit. Ah, judgmentalism, a particularly juicy fruit. Now if I am going to get my fruit-inspecting license, it helps to be objective. No better way to be objective than to have a checklist to go by. William Perkins, a Reformed scholar in the 18th Century, had a helpful list. One could determine the election of himself or someone else by observing the following fruit:

- Feelings of bitterness of heart when we have offended God by sin
- Striving against the flesh
- Desiring God's grace earnestly
- Considering that God's grace is a most precious jewel
- Loving the ministers of God's Word
- Calling upon God earnestly and with tears
- Desiring Christ's second coming
- Avoiding all occasions of sin
- Persevering in the effects to the last gasp of life.[3]

My favorite is the fifth one: gotta love pastors. I consigned anyone who didn't like me to the reprobate. Just kidding. But don't you just love the last one? If one of the fruits of the elect is to persevere in the effects of the faith until one's last gasp of life, then when will he know he is elect? Duh.

John MacArthur has another list, which he takes from 1 John:

- Have you enjoyed fellowship with Christ and the Father?
- Are you sensitive to sin?
- Do you obey God's Word?
- Do you reject this evil world?
- Do you eagerly await Christ's return?
- Do you see a decreasing pattern of sin in your life?
- Do you love other Christians?

- Do you experience answered prayer?
- Do you experience the ministry of the Holy Spirit?
- Can you discern between spiritual truth and error?
- Have you suffered rejection because of your faith?

MacArthur introduces this list with these words: "Throughout the letter [1 John] is a series of tests to determine whether you possess eternal life. If you don't pass these tests, you'll know where you stand and what you need to do."[4] Can you at least see why such a list could promote more doubt than assurance? Do I obey God's Word enough? Do I love other believers enough? Do I reject this present world enough? And on it goes.

FG theology delivers us from the fruit-inspecting industry. Fruit-inspecting involves judging other people, and Jesus had a lot to say about not judging other people (Matt 7:1-5; Jas 2:1-4; 4:11-12; 5:9).

FG theology promotes a love relationship with God.

Take the most famous Bible verse in the world, John 3:16—"For God so loved the world that He gave His only begotten Son . . ." In Reformed theology, these words are inserted into the verse: "of the elect"—the world of the elect. They believe God only loves the elect; He hates the reprobate (unbelievers). Christ died only for the elect (limited atonement). And since they also think the vast majority ("many are called but few are chosen") of everyone God created will spend eternity in hell/Lake of Fire, then God hates the vast majority of everyone He has or will create.

This view of a vengeful, hateful God is what turned Thomas Talbot, a leading proponent of Universalism, from Calvinism to Universalism. He told me he was singing a hymn in church one Sunday while still a teenager, and all of a sudden, he could not sing anymore. He could not worship a God who would knowingly create the vast majority of people to torture in hell for eternity.[5] But it doesn't have to be that way.

In my classes on soteriology (study of salvation), I sometimes ask a married man how long he and his wife dated before marriage. Usually, it is at least a year. "Did you take her out to eat or to a movie during that time?" Sure. "Well, if you thought she was the one you wanted, why didn't you just hit her on the head with a club and drag her off to your cave? You could have saved a lot of time and money." If they are slow with their answer, I will usually say, "Well, did you ask her to marry you?" Yes. "Why did you do that? Just bop her on the head and take her. Sure, save on wedding expenses." Finally, they will say something to the effect that they wanted her to have a choice. "Why? Why did you want her to have a choice?" Then they get it: if he did not give her a choice, he would never know if she loved him. "You mean you wanted her to love you?" Right. "Do you think God wants to be loved any less than we do? After all, God is love."

You see, if we take human choice away, God would never have external evidence that we love Him. If nothing else, the Bible is a love story. At the very heart of Deuteronomy is the shema, a statement uttered every day by religious Jews: "Love the Lord your God with all your heart, all your soul, and all your strength." And Jesus picked up on this, didn't He? "What's the greatest commandment?" the Pharisees ask. Then Jesus quotes the shema. But entities without choice are just that: entities, not people. The capacity to have volition is part of being created in the image of God. Take choice away, and we have robots. The deterministic system of Calvinism makes God sovereign over robots. God micromanaged every detail of a person's life. There are no free choices.

Every church father between 100 C.E. and 400 C.E. who wrote on the subject (fifty out of eighty) taught free choice for human beings.[6] It wasn't until around 400 C.E. when Augustine imported the determinism of Manichaeism, Neoplatonism, Gnosticism, and Stoicism into Christianity that any theologian excised the capacity to choose from mankind. The early church fathers did not agree on everything, but there is one thing they did agree on in their *Regula Fide* (Rule of Faith): even after the fall, men and women have the capacity to make choices. By taking that away, Augustine turned people into robots and God into a hateful, capricious Creator who takes pleasure in the suffering of those whom He has created. That venomous view bled over the Atlantic to American theologians like Jonathan Edwards, who wrote in his famous sermon, *Sinners in the Hands of an Angry God*:

The God that holds you over the pit of hell, much in the same way as one holds a spider, or some loathsome insect over the fire, abhors you, and is dreadfully provoked; his wrath towards you burns like fire; he looks upon you as worthy of nothing else but to be cast into the fire; he is of purer eyes than to bear to have you in his sight; you are ten thousand times more abominable in his eyes than the most hateful venomous serpent is in ours.[7]

Doesn't sound much like a loving God, does it? Obviously, theologians of this ilk have softened Edward's tones to make their view of God more palatable for 21st Century listeners. But it's like putting candy on a rotten apple: the core is still rotten. Theodore Beza, Calvin's successor, even made a chart to clarify their position:

Beza's Double Predestination[8]

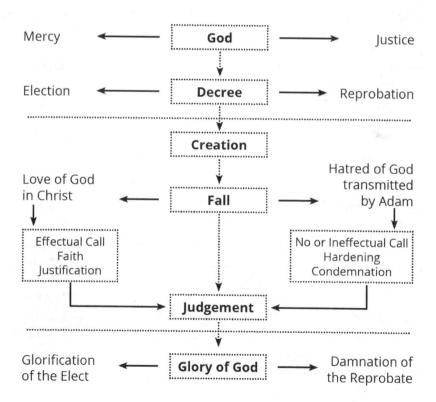

Notice God's hatred for the reprobate on the right side of the chart. He loves only the elect (left side). And since the vast majority of everyone He has or will create are reprobate, the logic is inescapable that God hates most of the people He has or will create. But this is so repulsive that some, like Rob Bell with his book *Love Wins*, have swung the pendulum to the other extreme. The love of God is so powerful that all created beings will spend eternity with God. That includes all human unbelievers, the fallen angels, and the devil himself. After all, if even one creature winds up in the Lake of Fire for eternity, then evil won instead of love.

Neither of these extremes is necessary. God is love, and He desires nothing more than a loving relationship with His human creatures. FG theology recognizes that and preserves the free choice within mankind that makes this kind of love relationship possible. Someone will say, but the Arminians hold the same view. In fact, their idea of sanctification is to be perfected in God's love. True, but FG theology teaches a stronger love than that of the Arminians. They teach the love relationship between the believer and God is lost if they don't persevere in the faith until the end of their lives. But FG theology teaches that "nothing can separate us from the love of Christ . . . neither things past nor things to come . . . " (Rom 8:38-39). In other words, there are no sins I can commit in the future ("things to come") that can separate me from God's love.

In FG theology, we believe entire books of the Bible (1 John) were written to promote a deeper love relationship with God.

FG theology offers greater motivation.

We have already talked about the joy of living a "thank-you" life instead of a "have-to" life. And gratitude is motive enough for many to live a godly life. But for some, God offers more. He encourages us to join the ranks of those who want to be in His army and make a difference in this world. He does not draft us; He invites us (Rom 12:1). It is a volunteer army (Ps 110:3). He warns us of the rigors and sacrifices of army life (Lk 14:26-32) and warns us of heading down the road of discipleship without counting the costs, which could be our very lives. But He also entices us.

Peter asked what he and the other disciples would get in the next life ("the regeneration") because they had left everything to follow Christ (Matt 19:27). Jesus tells them they will co-reign with Him when He sits on the throne of His glory. They will rule over the twelve tribes of Israel. We take this to mean during the Millennium (Christ's thousand-year reign on earth, see Rev. 20). Then Christ goes on to motivate others who have made sacrifices to be part of His army. They will get a hundred times whatever they have sacrificed. What is Christ doing here? Pretty obvious, isn't it? He is offering rewards to be given at the Judgment Seat of Christ to those who have sacrificed in this life to serve Him: "For we shall all stand before the judgment seat of Christ" (Rom 14:10c); and, "For we must all appear before the judgment seat of Christ, that each one may receive the things *done* in the body, according to what he has done, whether good or bad" (2 Cor 5:10).

I would go so far as to say that anticipation of future rewards is half of the motivation God uses to encourage us to join His army and to persevere when the going gets tough. It's all over the NT. Here are just a couple of passages:

"He who receives you receives Me, and he who receives Me receives Him who sent Me. He who receives a prophet in the name of a prophet shall receive a prophet's **REWARD**. And he who receives a righteous man in the name of a righteous man shall receive a righteous man's **REWARD**. And whoever gives one of these little ones only a cup of cold *water* in the name of a disciple, assuredly, I say to you, he shall by no means lose his **REWARD**." (Matt 10:40-42)

Then Jesus said to His disciples, "If anyone desires to come after Me, let him deny himself, and take up his cross, and follow Me. For whoever desires to save his life will lose it, but whoever loses his life for My sake will find it. For what profit is it to a man if he gains the whole world, and loses his own soul? Or what will a man give in exchange for his soul? For the Son of Man will come in the glory of His Father with His angels, and then He will **REWARD** each according to his works (Matt 16:24-27).

And behold, I am coming quickly, and My **REWARD** *is* with Me, to give to everyone according to his work (Rev 22:12).

And whatever you do, do it heartily, as to the Lord and not to men, knowing that from the Lord you will receive the **REWARD** of the inheritance; for you serve the Lord Christ (Col 3:23-24).

Now he who plants and he who waters are one, and each one will receive his own **REWARD** according to his own labor. For we are God's fellow workers; you are God's field, *you are* God's building. According to the grace of God which was given to me, as a wise master builder I have laid the foundation, and another builds on it. But let each one take heed how he builds on it. For no other foundation can anyone lay than that which is laid, which is Jesus Christ. Now if anyone builds on this foundation *with* gold, silver, precious stones, wood, hay, straw, each one's work will become clear; for the Day will declare it, because it will be revealed by fire; and the fire will test each one's work, of what sort it is. If anyone's work which he has built on *it* endures, he will receive a **REWARD**. If anyone's work is burned, he will suffer loss; but he himself will be saved, yet so as through fire (1 Cor 3:9-15).

For if I preach the gospel, I have nothing to boast of, for necessity is laid upon me; yes, woe is me if I do not preach the gospel! For if I do this willingly, I have a **REWARD**; but if against my will, I have been entrusted with a stewardship. What is my **REWARD** then? (1 Cor 9:16-18)

In FG theology we make a clear distinction between the "gift" and the "prize." The gift is the free gift of life with God forever. No works: "For by grace you have been saved through faith, and that not of yourselves; *it is* the **GIFT** of God" (Eph 2:8-9). But the prize is whatever God graciously decides to give those who sacrificially serve Him: "Do you not know that those who run in a race all run, but one receives the **PRIZE**? Run in such a way that you may obtain *it*" (1 Cor. 9:24). The gift excludes our works; the prize includes our works.

The reason this emphasis on rewards is unique to FG theology is because we in no way attach our good works to getting into heaven. We have seen that all theologies that require us to remain faithful and living a life of good works until the end of our time on earth in order to go to heaven when we die have made good works a requirement for eternal life. They confuse the gift and the prize. For them the gift is the prize. And in some of these theologies everyone gets the same reward because the only people who get to heaven are those who have persevered. Well, if all the elect have persevered faithfully until the end of their lives, then why wouldn't they all get the same rewards?[9]

Wayne Grudem has written the most popular one-volume book on systematic theology used by seminaries in America. It is over a thousand pages long. But he includes less than three pages on rewards for believers.[10] Why? Because they are not an emphasis in his theology. With this approach I would suggest that half the motivation for living the Christian life is lost.

Some people might object by saying, "Oh, rewards don't motivate me. The doctrine of rewards seems selfish. It's about me and my glory." That's a fair objection, but it betrays a misunderstanding. Rewards are not about me and my glory; they are about Christ and His glory. The Scripture gives us different metaphors to help us understand rewards: gold, silver, precious stones, crowns, wreaths, etc. But what do we do with the crowns we receive? We cast them at the feet of Christ (Rev 4:10), declaring that He alone is worthy to wear them, for without Him we could do nothing of eternal value (Jn 15:5).

Our rewards are a measure of how much glory we bring to our Savior forever. The more faithful we have been, the more glory we bring to Him. Daniel 12:3 tells us, "Those who are wise shall shine like the brightness of the firmament, and those who turn many to righteousness like the stars forever and ever." The simile used here is heavenly planets. What shine like stars but are not stars? Moons and planets. They have no light of their own; they just reflect the light of the star around which they revolve. So it is, as we revolve our lives around the Son, we, who have no light of our own, reflect His light. The more we become like Christ while on earth, the more of His character qualities we reflect, all unto His glory. What, after all, is the glory of God? It is the open manifestation of His attributes. The more we become like Him, the more of His attributes we manifest (reflect).

Do you find that selfish? For me it is one of the greatest motivations in the Christian life. There are so many times when I want to respond in an unloving way to someone who has hurt me in some way but becoming like Jesus is learning to love those who have hurt us. To retaliate is of the flesh and the devil; to forgive is from the Spirit and like Christ. When we do the kind of things Jesus did, we are becoming more like Him, and Daniel says we will reflect His character qualities forever. So, the greater the rewards, the greater the glory—for Him, not me.

FG theology provides better understanding through categories.

A frequent question often asked of pastors or seminary professors is: "If all my sins (past, present, and future) were forgiven at the cross, why do I have to ask for forgiveness when I sin?" It's a good question, isn't it? A similar question is raised by Luther's statement about being just and sinful at the same time (simul iustus et peccator). How can a person be justified and still be sinful? Or how can Paul say we are justified by faith without works and James say we are justified by faith and works? They can't both be right, can they?

Well, actually they can. The answers to these questions come when we learn to recognize different categories of truth. This chart shows some but not all of the categories:

RELATIONSHIP	FELLOWSHIP
POSITION	CONDITION
ETERNAL	TEMPORAL
JUSTIFICATION	SANCTIFICATION
SALVATION	REWARDS
ACCEPTANCE	APPROVAL
THE GIFT	THE PRIZE

Let's take the first question on forgiveness. The Bible presents the believer as part of a family. We have a spiritual Father, and we are His children. That is an eternal relationship. Some things are irreversible in life—like being born. Once a child is born physically, he can't be born physically again. It's a done deal—only going to happen once. And we don't have to be omniscient to know before they are born that our children are going to sin. So, what is our plan for them when they sin? Kick them out of the family? No. They have future forgiveness for their sins before they are born. Why? Because of our relationship: parent/child. The relationship is eternal.

However, if my child steals a hundred dollars from my wallet, and I find out about it, we have a problem. There is a personal offense. We are not going to be enjoying our eternal relationship. Our fellowship has been broken. The relationship is intact, but not the fellowship. In order to restore our fellowship, my son would need to come to me to ask for forgiveness. Of course, I would extend it to him. On what basis? On the basis of our eternal relationship: father/child.

The Scriptures speak of "relationship" forgiveness and "fellowship" forgiveness. We find the first in Ephesians 1:7 where Paul is enumerating all the spiritual blessings we have "in Christ" in heavenly places. When he writes of the blessings we have "in Christ," he is describing our "position;" we are "**in Him**." As such all our sins (past, present, and future) are forgiven: "**In Him** we have redemption through His blood, the forgiveness of sins, according to the riches of His grace." That is relationship forgiveness or forgiveness in our position.

But 1 John 1:9 explains "fellowship" forgiveness. The word "fellowship" is used four times in the first seven verses of this chapter. John's concern here is not establishing a "relationship" with God. The word "we" is used eighteen times in 1 John 1:1-2:2. In the first seven times, "we" refers to the apostles. But then John brings his readers into the fold, and in the next eleven times "we" is used, it includes the apostles and his readers. The point? These people are believers; they have an eternal "relationship" with God. But in order to maintain "fellowship" with God they need to walk in the light. If they do that, the blood of Jesus Christ will keep on cleansing them of the unknown sin in their life. Cleansing for what? Fellowship. But if they become aware of sin in their life, that fellowship is broken until they go to their heavenly Father and ask for His forgiveness. He is faithful and just to give it, for one reason, because on a relationship level, they already have advanced forgiveness of all their future sins. But the issue now is fellowship. That can only be restored by asking for forgiveness.

Understanding these different categories of truth can be very helpful in answering why many passages in Scripture that might appear to be contradictory are not contradictory at all. They are simply giving us truth in different categories. Let's look at one more: Position and Condition. Hebrews 10 puts these two categories side by side in verses ten and fourteen. Hebrews 10:10 says, "By that will we have been sanctified through the offering of the body of Jesus Christ once *for all*." When the writer wrote the word "sanctified," he put it in the perfect tense (*hagiasmenoi*), which carries the idea of action completed in the past with results extending to the present. So, he is saying we are completely sanctified right now through one sacrifice for all time. That's what Luther meant when he said we are *iustus* (just). We are completely sanctified in our Position in Christ in heavenly places. The Father on His throne puts on His Son glasses, and the red tint from His blood filters out all our sin. Our Father sees us as perfectly holy.

But we know we are not perfectly holy. We are aware of our sinful nature and the many times we fall into its clutches. Doesn't God see that? Of course, He does. But that is in our Condition here on earth. We have these twin truths juxtaposed: what's true in heaven and what's true on earth—at the same time. Got that? I don't. I'm not sure we can comprehend all that this means, but we can be encouraged by this: Hebrews 10:14 says, "For by one offering He has perfected forever those who are being sanctified." There's that word "sanctified" again. But this time it is not in the perfect tense. It doesn't speak of completed action in the past. It is in the present tense and speaks of the ongoing process of sanctification by which we are made progressively more and more like Christ (2 Cor 3:18). This is not a statement about our Position; it's a statement about our Condition.

It's hard to understand how we can be holy in our Position in heaven but unholy in our Condition on earth. But here is the beauty of FG theology. *Nothing in our Condition on earth can change our Position in heaven.* Our Position in heaven is completely secure while God continues to work on our Condition on earth—if we will let Him. We do not think our progressive sanctification on earth is guaranteed, as some theologies teach. The Calvinist claim that the progressive sanctification of the elect is guaranteed because a condition for being elect is that the believer will persevere faithfully until the end of his life. The Arminians do not think sanctification is guaranteed because they think you can forfeit your salvation through serious sin or not persevering. We don't say our sanctification is guaranteed because Paul says Hymenaeus and Alexander suffered shipwreck concerning their faith (1 Tim 1:19-20) and had to be turned over to Satan to teach (*paideuō*—a word consistently used of child training) them not to blaspheme. Demas went after this world (2 Tim 4:10) after serving with Paul off and on for a number of years. A brother can go astray and suffer a premature physical death (Jas 5:19-20).

God does not force us to become holy. But He will progressively make us holy if we don't quench the Spirit or resist the Spirit or grieve the Spirit. It is comforting to know that if I slip up, He doesn't kick me out of the family. The Father waits for His prodigal son. My Position in the family is secure. **Nothing I do in my Condition on earth can change my Position in heaven; but a focus on my Position in heaven can change my Condition on earth.** How? 2 Corinthians 3:18 says, "But we all, with unveiled face, beholding as in a mirror the glory of the Lord, are being transformed into the same image from glory to glory, just as by the Spirit of the Lord." This transformation is the sanctifying process of Hebrews 10:14. It's accomplished by the Spirit of the Lord. He is the Sculptor. Our responsibility? Behold the Lord. As we focus on our Position in heaven, the Spirit of the Lord is at work and transforms our Condition on earth. And when we focus on Jesus, we become like Jesus. **We become what we think about.** "For as he thinks in his heart, so is he" (Prov 23:7).

We propose that thinking in these categories will greatly increase our understanding of Scripture and the Christian life. In fact, Michael Eaton, who wrote *No Condemnation*, credits thinking in theological categories for much of the transformation in his own theology:

Whereas Arminianism and Calvinism—especially in their later forms—have thought of these two matters (salvation, reward) as so closely tied together has to make them virtually one category of thought, I conceive of them as decidedly two categories of thought. 1 Cor. 3:15 puts this in a nutshell: 'he shall suffer a loss . . . he shall be saved.' Reward may be lost, although salvation is retained. Thus, they should be thought of as two categories. The reassuring aspects of New Testament teaching concern *justification*. The admonitory aspects of New Testament teaching concern not justification or its loss, but *reward* and the possibility of loss of reward. The two matters may be kept distinct in our thinking.[11]

Space will not allow us to illustrate each category, but let me encourage you, when you are trying to understand a difficult passage, just start asking categorical questions:

- Is this talking about our Relationship or our Fellowship?
- Is this talking about our Position or our Condition?
- Is this talking about Temporal Judgment or Eternal Judgment?
- Is this talking about Justification or Sanctification?
- Is this talking about being saved from the Penalty of Sin or the Power of Sin?
- Is this talking about the Gift of salvation or the Prize of eternal rewards?
- Is this talking about Acceptance or Approval?

This is not an exhaustive list of categories. Nor is this a complete list of the ways FG theology can be a blessing. But hopefully these will amplify your own appreciation for the incredible grace given to each member of His family.

One final thought. Free Grace theology has been accused of being something new, concocted by a small splinter of people among evangelicals. It is really what traditional Southern Baptists have taught since their inception, despite the creeping influence of Reformed theology within the Southern Baptist ranks today. Free Grace theology reflects the doctrinal statement of Dallas Theological Seminary, especially their statement on assurance,[12] which says the new believer can have assurance as soon as he believes since his assurance is sourced in God's promise(s) instead of his own fruit. If it rested on his own fruit, the new believer could not have immediate assurance. As such, luminaries of the faith like Lewis Sperry Chafer, Dwight Pentecost, and Charles Ryrie were proponents of what we are calling Free Grace theology for decades before the MacArthur/Hodges flap. So, while the moniker is new, the theology is not.

Free Grace theology does not add any mixture of faith and works: you "have to do" any works before you believe or after you believe to have the gates of heaven opened for you. In other words, there is no "front-end" load or "back-end" load on the gospel of faith. Just believe. Furthermore, neither works nor perseverance in good works is made part of the makeup of faith. To repeat, works are not required before faith, in faith, or after faith in the person and work of Jesus. That's why we can live a "thank-you life" instead of a "have-to life." The former brings joy; the latter can turn the Christian life into a job instead of a joy.

Free Grace Theology is also the only theology that promises present assurance of our salvation because it does not depend on perseverance in good works until the end of our physical lives on earth to go to heaven, as does Catholicism, Calvinism, and Arminianism. This assurance brings an abiding peace on the saint who still finds himself sinning after years in the faith.

In summation, Free Grace Theology truly is good news. Because we live a "thank-you life" instead of a "have-to life" we find joy even in tough times that comes to the volunteer as opposed to a draftee. Because we do not have to persevere in good works until the end of our lives on earth, we have the abiding peace that results from having the assurance of our salvation. Because our assurance does not depend on our own good fruit, we can be free from the depressing task of fruit inspecting: our own or that of others. Because our lives are not predetermined, we can also enjoy an intimate love relationship with our Savior that comes from our choices to obey His commandments and thus demonstrate that we love Him and, in return, bathe in His love for us as He manifests Himself to us (Jn 14:21). Because God motivates us with rewards according to our faithfulness that will accrue to His glory for all eternity, there is greater impetus to remain true to Him despite our current suffering. And finally, because Free Grace Theology helps us think in categories of truth, we are better able to explain some of the apparent contradictions in Scripture.

Truly there are many other benefits of Free Grace Theology which are not written in this book; but these are written that you may believe that Jesus is the Christ, the Son of God, and that by believing you may have life in His name.

Bibliography

Anderson, Dave. *Free Grace Soteriology*. 3rd ed. Grace Theology Press, 2019.

Bing, Charlie. *Grace, Salvation & Discipleship: How to Understand Some Difficult Bible Passages*. Grace Theology Press, 2015.

Chay, Fred, ed. *A Defense of Free Grace Theology: With Respect to Saving Faith, Perseverance, and Assurance*. Grace Theology Press, 2017.

---

[1] Augustine, *Aurelius, The Works of Aurelius Augustine, Volume 15: The Anti-Pelagian Works*, ed. M. Dods (Edinburgh: T and T Clark,1876). The Latin title is *De Domo Perseverantiae*, "On the Benefit of Perseverance." 21.8.

[2] Michael Eaton wrote a book for popular audiences based on his dissertation: *No Condemnation: A New Theology of Assurance* (Downers Grove, IL: InterVarsity, 1995).

[3] William Perkins, *The Works of William Perkins*, vol. 1 (Grand Rapids: Reformation Heritage Books, 2014), 115.

[4] John MacArhtur, Jr., *Saved without a Doubt* (Colorado Springs, CO: Chariot Victor Publishing, 1992), 68-91.

[5] Thomas Talbott. This came from a personal interview in July, 2015. He wrote *The Inescapable Love of God* (Universal Publishers/uPUBLISH.com, 1999) as his defense of universalism (that all of God's creatures including the fallen angels and the devil will be with God for eternity).

[6] Kenneth M. Wilson, *Augustine's Conversion from Traditional Free Choice to "Non-Free Free Will": A Comprehensive Methodology* (Tüningen: Mohr Siebeck, 2018), 41-94.

[7] "Sinners in the Hands of an Angry God," *Wikisource*, https://en.wikisource.org/wiki/Sinners_in_the_Hands_of_an_Angry_God, accessed September 23, 2020.

[8] In *Summa totius Christianismi*, Quellenverzeichnis Nr. 6. Translation mine.

[9] John Piper, *Suffering and the Sovereignty of God* (Wheaton: Crossway Books, 2006), 94-95. Piper contradicts himself here when he says the Christian who suffers for Christ will be rewarded with more glory than the one who does not suffer, but goes on in the same discussion to say he does not believe in different levels of rewards in the next life.

[10] Wayne Grudem, *Systematic Theology* (Grand Rapids, MI: Zondervan Publishing House, 1994), 1143-45.

[11] Eaton, 39.

[12] "Doctrinal Statement," *Dallas Theological Seminary*, https://www.dts.edu/about/doctrinal-statement/assurance, accessed October 7, 2020. "We believe it is the privilege, not only of some, but of all who are born again by the Spirit through faith in Christ as revealed in the Scriptures, to be assured of their salvation from the very day they take Him to be their Savior and that this assurance is not founded upon any fancied discovery of their own worthiness or fitness, but wholly upon the testimony of God in His written Word . . ."

Chapter 2

Practicing Grace in Ministry

Dr. Charles C. Bing

When we speak of ministry, we are not talking about selfish prestige and power or dominance over others. Reflected in some of the biblical words that describe those who minister, the prominent idea is service to others.[1] We should view any position of service as a gift of God's grace and treat it accordingly as stewards of that grace (Rom 1:5; 1 Cor 15:10; Eph 3:7; 1 Pet 4:10). Serving others will require resources beyond most human capability. But grace covers our inadequacies as well (2 Cor 3:5-6). So like salvation and all of the Christian life, ministry begins and is sustained by grace.

Grace is not only a theological term that helps us understand how God shares His unconditional love towards us, it is also a moral term that should influence our conduct, especially in ministry. Serving others is most effective when it reflects the unconditional love and grace of our God through His Son, Jesus Christ, who Himself is described as "full of grace and truth" (John 1:14).

All Christians are called to love and serve the needs of others. This makes all believers ministers in a sense (Eph 4:12). But we also recognize that some believers are uniquely gifted to serve by leading, preaching, teaching, shepherding, evangelizing, and going cross-culturally as missionaries. Let's talk about how grace impacts these different arenas of service.

Grace in one-another ministry

Ministry is as close as the person next to you as indicated by the many "one another" commands for those in the Body of Christ. But the premier command, the new and great command that accompanies the priority of our love for God, is "Love one another" (Matt. 22:37-39; John 13:34-35; 1 John 3:11, 23). The word used for love, *agapē*, signals an unconditional, unselfish love that seeks the best for others. When we love, we reflect the love that God has for us and all people (1 John 4:19). But that love has to be communicated through His grace—the free gift of His resources to meet any need, beginning with our salvation. The old hymn reminds us,

> *Oh, the love that drew salvation's plan!*
>
> *Oh, the grace that brought it down to man!*
>
> *Oh, the mighty gulf that God did span at Calvary!* (William R. Newell, *At Calvary*)

After the grace of God is given, it begins a transforming process of training us to live godly lives:

> [11]*For the grace of God that brings salvation has appeared to all men,* [12]*teaching us that, denying ungodliness and worldly lusts, we should live soberly, righteously, and godly in the present age.* (Titus 2:11-12)

God trains us in righteousness by His Spirit using His Word, but also by His Spirit using other believers. That's where we come in to serve. Each believer is uniquely gifted by God's grace to minister to others:

> *As each one has received a gift, minister it to one another, as good stewards of the manifold grace of God.* (1 Pet 4:10)

At the top of God's list is the command to love one another. Loving others is not easy. It means accepting people as they are and trying to see them as God sees them in the present moment and in the potential future. I admit that I have seen some people living so diametrically opposed to God's desires that I gave up hope for them. I also admit that I have been pleasantly surprised when I heard of some of these people turning their lives around to love and serve God. Thank God His love is more tenacious than mine!

Our gracious love for others can manifest itself in many ways that reflect God's love and grace. Some of the ways listed in the New Testament are:

- Be kindly affectionate to one another. Rom 12:10

- Be patient and kind to one another. 1 Cor 13:4

- Serve one another. Gal 5:13

- Restore those who sin. Gal 6:1

- Bear one another's burdens. Gal 6:2

- Forgive one another. Eph 4:32

- Submit to one another. Eph 5:21

- Comfort and edify one another. 1 Thess 5:11

- Pray for each other. Jas 5:16

When dealing with others, one particular area that needs a lot of grace is the issue of gray areas or questionable practices. I am talking about making choices that are not directed by any clear scriptural teaching. This was evidently a problem for churches under the apostle Paul's oversight since he addressed major sections of his epistles to it (Rom 14:1–15:6; 1 Cor 10:23-33). Issues he dealt with in the early churches included observing certain holidays, eating certain foods, and drinking wine. Modern comparisons might be issues about the propriety of observing certain traditions associated with holidays like Christmas, Easter, or Halloween, or whether it is permissible for Christians to drink alcoholic beverages, get a tattoo, or watch certain movies and television shows. Christians hold different opinions about these things, so how should we conduct ourselves towards those with whom we disagree? One course could lead to license where anything is permissible under grace regardless of how it affects me or others. Another course could lead to legalism where activities are condemned without clear biblical warrant. Under grace we are indeed free, but that freedom should be used to serve God and benefit others with love as our chief motive (Gal 5:13). Not license, not legalism, but liberty controlled by love.

In his epistles, the apostle Paul gives some principles that can help us make wise choices and show others grace in questionable issues:

- Do only that which will edify, not enslave you. 1 Cor 6:12; 10:23

- Do not do anything that will hurt or hinder another Christian. Rom 14:19-21; 1 Cor 8:9-13; 10:24-29

- Do not despise or show contempt toward your fellow Christian about a questionable practice. Rom 14:3,10

- Do not judge fellow Christians, because they must give an account for their behavior before God at the Judgment Seat of Christ. Rom 14:10-13

- Do everything to the glory of God. 1 Cor 10:30-31

- Do not do anything to tarnish your witness to unbelievers. 1 Cor 10:32-33

We can also demonstrate grace to others, especially those in need, by generous giving. When we give, we should first consider what God has given to us in Jesus Christ. We give to others as God has graciously given to us (2 Cor 8:9; 9:6-15). True gracious giving is not motivated by outside pressure, but by inner gratitude (2 Cor 9:7). Sometimes this "grace giving" can be funneled through the church's general fund, given to a special fund, or given directly to the person(s) in need. Throughout our years of ministry, Karen and I have been surprised by financial gifts or provisions that were often given anonymously. Many times, we did not know how we would pay for tuition, rent, or car repairs, but just when it was needed, a gift would arrive. We thanked God for such generosity and to this day remain sensitive to the needs of others so that we can share the same grace of giving.

There is so much more that could be said about how to show grace in the Christian community. In general, we treat others as Jesus Christ treats us. He accepts us unconditionally as His children regardless of race, color, culture, sinful tendencies, and peculiarities. He is patient with us and gives us room to grow in grace. It is the attitude and the enablement of God's grace that will help us in our differences and our attitudes towards other believers in the church community.

Grace in pastoral ministry

Whether called pastor or elder, those who shepherd others have a special privilege of serving people by providing leadership, oversight, instruction, exhortation, comfort, and by responding to needs. Only those shepherds who know they are secure in God's grace will be free to minister to others with the same grace.

The positions of pastor and elder are those of exemplary servanthood rather than domination:

> [2]*Shepherd the flock of God which is among you, serving as overseers, not by compulsion but willingly, not for dishonest gain but eagerly;* [3]*nor as being lords over those entrusted to you, but being examples to the flock.* (1 Pet 5:2-3).

The secure acceptance with God provided by His grace should keep shepherds from trying to control people with fear or rules. Those under their care are also recipients of God's grace. Shepherds want to see their people grow and prosper spiritually, but that life-change must not be coerced by external pressure, guilt, or fear. The grace-guided pastor understands that the best motivation for change is helping others appreciate the love and grace of God so that they will live gratefully for Him.

It is helpful to see how the apostle Paul uses two analogies to describe his ministry of grace towards the Thessalonian church, which we can assume would describe his general attitude towards all the churches in his charge. He shepherded the Thessalonian church with the gentleness of a nursing mother who cherishes her children. That included his affectionate longing for them and the sharing of his life with them. He also related to them as a father would his children by exhorting, comforting, and charging them with responsibilities (1 Thess 2:7-11). Shepherds of God's people would do well to imitate Paul's parental model of ministry. Parents naturally understand the necessity of showing grace to their children.

God's grace provides what leaders need. The Bible is full of accounts of people called to lead who felt inadequate (e.g., Moses, Gideon, Solomon, the twelve disciples) but were able to accomplish their tasks with God's help. I call this "unwanted grace"—God provides what we need when He asks us to do something we don't think we can do. Ministry is when God asks us to do what we cannot do with resources we do not have. But God can do anything through us with the infinite resources grace provides. It takes God's grace to lead others in dependence upon Him and do it with a servant's attitude.

Pastoral ministry is difficult and taxing. I speak from 25 years of pastoral ministry, 19 of those years as lead pastor of a church plant. Pastors must take the time to study God's Word afresh each week and shape it into a message that people can use. The weekly grind of message preparation alone is crushing, but they also have to mentor and disciple other church leaders and servants. Then there are endless meetings and endless things to pray about. Pastors are on call 24 hours a day regardless of how tired they might be. As if present issues in the church are not enough, pastors must also lead by envisioning the future for their church. On top of all this, pastors must not only endure but love critical and unpleasant people. Now how can a pastor do all this except by the grace of God?

In his ministry, the apostle Paul realized that his inadequacies were covered by the grace of God. When speaking of his ministry, which was always under attack, he asks, "Who is sufficient for such things?" (2 Cor 2:16). He then answers,

> [5]*Not that we are sufficient of ourselves to think of anything as being from ourselves, but our sufficiency is from God,* [6]*who also made us sufficient as ministers of the new covenant, not of the letter but of the Spirit; for the letter kills, but the Spirit gives life.* (2 Cor 3:5-6)

In the face of difficult pastoral ministry, Paul exhorts Timothy, "You therefore, my son, be strong in the grace that is in Christ Jesus" (2 Tim 2:1). Pastors must rely on the sufficiency of God's grace.

Perhaps grace is most needed in one of a pastor's most unpleasant tasks—dealing with those who go astray. Pastors who balance grace with truth will lovingly confront those who sin and, if necessary, lovingly subject them to church discipline. Grace should temper how a pastor deals with sinning believers because it reminds him that God accepted him with all his faults as much as God still loves and accepts those who sin. Shepherds who understand the realities of sin, Satan, and the weakness of our flesh will not simply dismiss those who sin as unsaved (though that may be a possibility), but if they have a clear testimony of faith in Christ, will appeal to them on the basis of how they should live in response to God's love and the grace they have received. The Scriptures remind us that there is no sin that is beyond God's forgiveness and restoration: "where sin abounded, grace abounded much more" (Rom 5:20).

Another pressure pastors face is the pressure to perform and grow the church numerically. Many pastors dread answering the question, "How many people do you have?" They don't enjoy playing the comparison game. Under grace, pastors should get their sense of significance not from how they are doing but from who they are in Christ and whether they are faithful to the ministry they have been given. Think of the church issues that the apostle Paul faced: criticism, alienation, betrayal, and subterfuge, yet he did not consider his ministry a failure. He knew that as he labored, God labored in and with him: *"But by the grace of God I am what I am, and his grace toward me was not in vain; but I labored more abundantly than they all, yet not I, but the grace of God which was with me"* (1 Cor 15:10). He was able to say at the end of his ministry, *"I have fought the good fight, I have finished the race, I have kept the faith"* (2 Tim 4:7). Paul was not exalting in his success because he knew that grace was his enablement.

Pastors and shepherds face extraordinary and seemingly impossible demands. But that is exactly the kind of situation God wants them in so that they can appreciate His all-sufficient grace.

Grace in preaching and teaching

Communicating God's Word to others is a great privilege and responsibility. Whether preaching or teaching, the goal is to convey truth accurately and transform lives toward Christlikeness. But grace has to start with the communicator. Grace is needed to study and understand God's Word. It is also needed to communicate it clearly and apply it lovingly. The more we have applied grace to our lives, the more effectively we can apply it to others. Grace allows us to magnify Christ and minimize our own importance: *"For we do not preach ourselves, but Christ Jesus the Lord, and ourselves your bondservants for Jesus' sake"* (2 Cor 4:5).

Those who preach and teach (and we could include those who write) are in a position of influence. That influence can be used either to coerce or to coax. Misdirected communicators will be tempted to coerce people to modify their behavior by preaching fear and false guilt. This plays on the natural tendency of most to think they are not doing enough for the Lord already. This can bring about outward conformity but may not bring about the inner transformation that comes from responding to God from love and gratitude. The impression left is that God will not accept the listener unless he does more or does better. Deserved guilt may motivate people to repent, confess their sin, and change, but evoking guilt unbiblically becomes spiritual abuse when people are told constantly that they are not doing enough to please God. We violate God's grace by preaching that His acceptance is based on their performance instead of their position as His children.

A better approach is to help people understand all that God in His grace has done for them and how He has blessed them with a new position in Christ and as His children. Then the speaker can coax the listeners to live up to their special position in Christ, or to "walk worthy of the calling by which you are called" (Eph 4:1). Consider how the apostle Paul motivated his readers in Romans, 1 Corinthians, and other epistles by teaching them how they are blessed by God's grace and given a new position *before* he tells them how they can please God by what they do. We find this pattern of explaining position before exhorting practice in a number of Paul's epistles.

Paul's Epistle	The Believer's Position Explained	The Believer's Practice Exhorted
Romans	Chapters 1-11	Chapters 12-15
Galatians	Chapters 1-4	Chapters 5-6
Ephesians	Chapters 1-3	Chapters 4-6
Colossians	Chapters 1-2	Chapters 3-4

We can look more closely at several clear and specific examples of this methodology. Paul's familiar appeal for Christians to "offer your body a living sacrifice" in Romans 12:1 is based on all that he has explained to them about God's grace in Romans chapters 1-11 ("in view of God's mercy" looks back to those chapters). Likewise, it is obvious in Ephesians 4:1 that the exhortation to "walk worthy of the calling by which you are called" reminds the readers of the preceding three chapters where Paul explains how God's grace has blessed them. In a similar way, the author of Hebrews uses a cyclical pattern as he explains the future rewards that God promises before he warns and exhorts his readers. For example, the explanations of the believer's position in Christ explained in chapter 1 is followed by the warnings and exhortations in chapters 2-3, and so on.

What can we learn from this pattern used by the authors of the epistles? We should preach the blessings of grace before we solicit the behavior of our listeners. Yet how often do we hear preaching that begins by telling the people that they need to do more of this or that? A threat of God's disfavor or judgment usually accompanies such preaching and occasionally a reminder of God's reward may be tacked on at the end. This methodology does not encourage the change motivated by an appreciation for what God has done for the listener. Remember, it is grace that trains us (Titus 2:11-12) by motivating us to live up to the blessings we have received. Preaching that emphasizes a list of things we should do is more fitting for living under the law than grace. But the Scriptures teach clearly that we are not under the law, but under grace (Rom 6:15).

Another opportunity for preachers and teachers to show grace is when they must defend the truth against those who would distort it. I'm not talking so much about outright heresy, because that should be condemned in the strongest terms. But believers can have different interpretations and views about many things that are not essential issues. Name calling, ridicule, ad hominem attacks, misrepresentation, and straw men arguments are not gracious. As preachers and teachers, we must learn to attack ideas, not people. Having said that, there are some occasions when people are so dangerous doctrinally or morally, that we must warn people away from them. On other occasions, we must simply and gently correct a teacher's erroneous views. Consider the example of Priscilla and Aquilla correcting Apollos on his deficient teaching (Acts 18:24-26). They did not condemn him as a false teacher but came alongside to help him have a better understanding of the truth, and all three continued on in fruitful ministry.

I have been preaching and teaching (and writing) for over 35 years. I am the first to admit I am helpless without God's enabling grace. As a grade school student, I could not stand before a class and talk without turning beet red and having severe stage fright. Maybe one difference is that now I have something to say that outweighs my fear. But I still feel the same anxiety before I speak or teach publicly. The main difference is that now I look to God's gracious provision for ideas, for insight, fruitful study, helpful messages, the right tone, boldness, and humility. I never speak or write a word that is not preceded by my prayers for these things.

People will be attracted to and transformed by preachers and teachers who preach grace graciously. It is a ministry that is both a privilege and a responsibility. As communicators of God's Word to God's people, I believe both our truth and our tone will be evaluated at the Judgment Seat of Christ (Jas 3:1; 2 Cor 5:9-10).

Grace in evangelism

Evangelism refers to spreading the gospel. When we talk about evangelism, it is tempting to talk about how we do it, but before we discuss methods, we should discuss the message.

Gospel means "good news." Only the gospel of God's free grace is good news. It is good news that God has done everything necessary to accomplish our salvation. He sent His Son, the Lord Jesus Christ, to pay the penalty for our sins with His death on a cross. Then Jesus rose from the dead as a living Savior to offer His eternal salvation to anyone who believes in Him for it. Since God in Christ has done all the work, all that is left for anyone to "do" is to believe. The gospel of grace makes no demands of the unsaved person except to believe in Jesus Christ for eternal salvation.

In much of evangelism today, this message has been perverted to include conditions other than believe. The unsaved person is told to do various things like make Jesus the Master of your life, commit your life to Christ, ask Jesus into your heart, turn from your sins, put Jesus on the throne of your life, be baptized, keep the commandments, and so on. Anything a person must do besides believe perverts the gospel of grace. I understand repentance as a change of mind about whatever is keeping someone from salvation and in that sense, belief encompasses such a change of thinking. The important thing is that repentance is an inner change, although that inner change should lead to an outward change (Matt 3:8/Luke 3:8; Acts 26:21).

Since God has made the gospel free—simply by grace through faith, the priority in grace-based evangelism should be to keep the gospel clear (Col 4:3-4). This means that we communicate the gospel of salvation by grace through faith alone in Christ alone. To understand they have a need for eternal salvation, unbelievers need to know that sin has separated them from God and their lack of belief in God's provision can keep them from His presence forever. They need to know that Jesus is the Son of God who died to pay the penalty for their sins and rose from the dead to offer eternal salvation with the gift of His life. They need to understand that "believe" is the single unencumbered condition for receiving that eternal salvation. To clarify this condition with them, it should be emphasized that anything added to "believe" negates God's free grace and makes salvation earned by performance, which is an impossibility according to Ephesians 2:8-9. In our evangelistic invitations, we must be careful not to use confusing terms, illustrations, and jargon so commonly heard that negate faith alone in Christ alone. One African evangelist told me after attending our conference on the gospel of grace, "I have to repent—I think I have been keeping people out of heaven by the many things I told them they have to do to be saved!" No wonder there are serious warnings for those who change the gospel (Gal 1:8-9)!

Only when we share this gospel of grace can people be saved and assured of their salvation. When sharing our message of salvation through faith alone, we can have the utmost confidence that it is the only message that guarantees eternal life unconditionally. Frankly, it is deceptive to offer anything called *"eternal* life" under conditions that include human works or merit. Nothing eternal can depend on our efforts. An evangelist with such a feeble message is more foolish than bold.

There is only one gospel message, but there can be many methods and ways to share it. Just make sure your method does not obscure the message. There are some popular presentations for sharing the gospel that misuse Scripture and illustrations. Many good presentations end with an invitation that contradicts the grace of God's work in salvation by asking the unsaved person to do something besides believe. Even the notion of "Pray this prayer to be saved" adds to simple faith. In whatever way you present the gospel, be sure to use Scripture, illustrations, and an invitation correctly. You can use some of the popular presentations if you modify them to keep grace free and faith simple. Some of my favorite passages that make the condition of faith alone clear and simple are John 3:16, 18; 4:10 (if you explain that "ask" is an analogy for "believe"); 5:24; 6:40, 47; 11:25-26; 20:30-31; Acts 16:30-31; Romans 3:21-24; Galatians 2:16; and Ephesians 2:8-9.

It is not just our presentation of the gospel that should reflect grace, but our motives and manner in evangelism must also show the grace of our Lord. As hard as it is to digest, some people preach the gospel for selfish gain or out of a spirit of contention and competition (Phil 1:15-17). The apostle Paul serves as a model for how we should avoid the appearance of financially profiting from preaching the gospel. It is better not to take any money at all if it casts aspersions on our motives for evangelism (1 Cor 9:8-18). Neither would Paul take shortcuts to achieve results by mishandling the Word of God (2 Cor 4:2; 1 Thess 2:4-6). Aberrations, like the prosperity gospel which promises health and wealth to those who believe, do not reflect the unselfish grace of God, but the selfish greed of mankind.

As we evangelize, our attitude and conduct must reflect grace. We cannot view ourselves as better than those who have not yet believed. We remember that we were in the same hopeless situation until we believed the gospel. As the popular cliché goes, we are as beggars offering bread to other beggars. The gospel does not make us inherently better than unbelievers; it only makes us forgiven, and that by no merit of our own. If anything, the gospel should humble us so that we should extend the gospel to others with humility. When our conduct and words are tempered by grace, we will attract people rather than repel them (Col 4:6).

The realization that our "God of all grace" (1 Pet 5:10) loves all people and wants them to hear the gospel and be saved should compel us to share the gospel message with everyone (2 Cor 5:14-15; 1 Tim 2:3-6), including those of every race, color, and creed in every part of the world. Consider how Jesus evangelized Samaria by transgressing social and religious prohibitions. In John 4 we see Him crossing geographical boundaries, gender boundaries, religious boundaries, and racial boundaries as he brought the gospel to the Samaritans through a sinful woman. God desires that all people be saved, but He has designed to do that through us. That means we should reflect His same passion for sharing the gospel. It also means that we should never impede or hinder His gospel by apathy or a lack of clarity. It would be incongruous for the God of all grace and we who are saved by grace to demand a cost for His salvation.

Evangelism is the human side of bringing people to salvation, but there is also a divine side. We understand that salvation by grace also means that God is working to convince people of the truth through the Holy Spirit to bring them to faith (John 6:44; 16:8-11; 2 Cor 4:1-6). We simply cooperate with His Spirit by our willingness to go and witness. This divine element makes prayer for the unsaved paramount. We should ask God that the light of His gospel would penetrate the blindness of the lost (2 Cor 4:3-4). Following Paul's example, we can also pray or ask for prayer for boldness (Eph 6:18-19), opportunities (Col 4:3), and clarity (Col 4:4).

Under grace, we who evangelize must accept unbelievers as God does and allow God to change them after they believe. We do not preach that life change is necessary to receive salvation. That is not only a false gospel but misunderstands the transformational power of grace when it touches a life. As someone has said, you do not clean fish before you catch them, but afterward.

To summarize, grace in evangelism is demonstrated with a clear and free gospel, pure motives, blameless conduct, a humble attitude, a passion to share with everyone, and prayerful dependence on God.

Grace in missions

Missions is the sending and going of Christ's disciples to other cultures to help spread the gospel and its grace. There is a growing trend among churches to define missions as local outreach and social involvement, but that is better understood as evangelism or outreach. I believe that when missions is everything, then missions is nothing.[2]

Those who minister in cultures other than their own, especially cultures outside of American evangelicalism, will find a world confused with a false "gospel" of works. I speak from the experience of ministering in almost twenty different countries. My conclusion from ministering in those countries is that our priority should be grounding people in the gospel of grace. There is much we can teach after that, and to be sure, there is a great need to know other subjects, but grace is foundational to salvation, assurance, and Christian growth. Since the Christian life begins and continues by grace, it is a crucial prism that colors how one views the Scriptures, other people, and the world.

A gospel of works and legalism traps people in uncertainty and the fear of condemnation. Assurance of salvation is impossible. Only by understanding the grace message will believers have a secure foundation for growing in grace.

It is probably easier to introduce the gospel of grace in cultures that have had no gospel witness at all. I like to echo a maxim that a friend, Ed Underwood, shares from his stint in the military in tank warfare: *Those who fire the first shot win the battle.* If we get there first, the hearers have no erroneous ideas about the Christian message or contrary theological baggage. On the other hand, in many places the people know enough about Christianity to be "dangerous," that is, they have assumptions about the gospel and the Christian life which hinder their comprehension of God's free grace. I find that a good exposition of a key book about the gospel like John, Romans or Galatians is very powerful and convincing. Instead of arguing against erroneous views that are usually supported by proof-texting, teaching these books presents a logical, coherent, and air-tight argument for salvation and sanctification by grace.

The task of those in missions it to learn the world view of other cultures so that both message and ministry can be more effective. Many times, those in the major religions of the world are in bondage to fear and the futility of their imperfect performance. Take the very popular concept of karma as an example. Karma is a closed system of justice where doing good earns more good and doing bad earns more bad. But the Bible teaches that God freely gives good (grace) to those who do bad (sin). As with all other works-based religions, karma provides the perfect environment to introduce the certainty and security of the gospel and its message of grace. To be sure, there will be some who resist and ask many questions, but I have found that persistence and the proper approach can bring many into the freedom of grace. Grace is so contradictory to their nature and their religious training that it may take years and constant repetition before they get it. The grace of patience is a needed virtue in missionary work.

Those from a developed western country who work in less developed nations can easily succumb to a superiority complex. I have seen this, and it is ugly. A condescending attitude towards nationals will seep into one's leadership style, relationships, message, and ultimately one's influence, which will be diminished. If the missions worker is from a developed nation, he or she had nothing to do with it; it is by God's grace. This should keep every missionary humble. Grace is needed to see the multitudes trapped in poverty and false religions as those loved by God as much as anyone else.

Since cultures and worldviews vary greatly, the emphasis of our cross-cultural message and ministry should be the essential truths of God's Word. The gospel is the same for everyone, though it may need to be explained and illustrated according to the targeted culture. This is also true of other essential doctrines. But there are many non-essential beliefs and practices that can be addressed later. Missionaries must work hard to observe and understand these different issues in the context of the various cultures and backgrounds. It requires much patience to learn cultural perspectives on leadership, money, worship, church rituals, etc.

Those in missions work will usually find themselves in a position of great need. Leaving the familiarity of their home culture, friends, language, housing, safety, technology, food, and other comforts, they will be challenged to adjust and adapt. This keeps the missionary in constant dependence on God's grace to provide what is needed. One of the things that I like most about cross-cultural ministry is exactly that—I cannot control very much so I have to depend on God and therefore get to see Him work. It is an exciting approach to life that is not always offered when living in our comfort zones.

Another need for grace on the mission field is working with other missionaries and the locals. People will be people--with all their imperfections and idiosyncrasies that seem amplified when living together in a confined environment. This brings us back to the necessity to show love and grace to one another. Practicing grace is the only way to survive the interpersonal and cultural challenges unique to the mission field.

Conclusion

Practicing grace in ministry is important because it changes us and others. As God's love and grace permeate and change us, our Christlikeness will overflow to serve others. We should learn to inspire others to godly living and service with the highest of motivations, beginning with love and gratitude to God for all that He has done. We must constantly remind one another of all that God has freely given us by His grace. The disciplines of discipleship will fade in the believer's life without these heartfelt motives that pull one forward into maturity.

Ministry to others is full of challenges and needs that exceed our capabilities. Those in ministry should hold closely the precious promise of Hebrews 4:16: *"Let us therefore come boldly to the throne of grace, that we may obtain mercy and find grace to help in time of need."*

Bibliography

Bing, Charles C. *Simply by Grace*. Grand Rapids: Kregel Publications, 2009.

Getz, Gene A. *Elders and Leaders: God's Plan for Leading the Church*. Chicago: Moody Publishers, 2003.

Lawrence, Bill. *Effective Pastoring: Giving Vision, Direction, and Care to your Church*. Nashville: Word Publishing, 1999.

Moyer, R. Larry. *Free and Clear: Understanding & Communicating God's Offer of Eternal Life*. Grand Rapids: Kregel Publications, 1997.

Spitters, Denny and Mathew Ellison. *When Everything is Missions*. Amazon Kindle edition, 2017.

---

[1] For example, in 1 Cor 3:5 "ministers," or *diakonoi*, is from *diakoneō* which means to serve; in 1 Cor 3:9 "fellow workers," or *synergoi*, is from *synergeō* which means *to work together*; in 1 Cor 4:1 "servants," or *hypēretas*, is from *hypēreteō* which means *to serve, be helpful*; in 1 Cor 4:1 "stewards," or *oikonomous*, is from *oikonomeō* which means *to manage*. These definitions can be found in Walter Bauer, William F. Arndt, and F. Wilbur Gingrich, *A Greek-English Lexicon of the New Testament and Other Early Christians Literature*, 3rd ed., rev. Frederick W. Danker (Chicago: University of Chicago Press, 2000).

[2] See Denny Spitters and Matthew Ellison, *When Everything is Missions* (Amazon Kindle edition), 2017.

Chapter 3

Parenting with Grace

Philip Congdon, Th.M.

Unless the Lord builds the house,
They labor in vain who build it.

Psalm 127:1

God's Sufficient Grace for an Impossible Task

The Perfect Family. Like a mirage in the desert, every young couple envisions future fulfillment and happiness on their wedding day, or when their first child is born. I don't want to burst your bubble, but the perfect family doesn't exist, and every parent faces struggles. Even Hollywood couldn't make the perfect family. We think of *Leave It to Beaver* or *The Brady Bunch* as idyllic families, but even they weren't perfect, and those days are a distant memory.

Parenting has always been one of the most daunting tasks facing God's people, and while it is more so today than in the past, history shows it has never been easy. Adam and Eve, the only humans to live in a sinless world, endured the agony of their first son, Cain, taking the life of their second, Abel. The pages of Scripture are littered with dysfunctional families. Israel's Patriarchs, Abraham, Isaac, and Jacob, and other 'heroes of faith' like Eli, Samuel, and David all have their parental failures recorded in the Bible.

And yet, despite all their foibles, God used these, and countless other imperfect dads and moms, in the unfolding of His gracious plan to save fallen humanity. Broken people, broken marriages, and broken homes were time and again redeemed and restored by the persistent grace of God. Our unchanging God is still in the business of redeeming brokenness today. If you are a parent, you have felt like a failure more than once. As Howard Hendricks so aptly put it, "The problem with being a parent is that when you finally feel competent, you're out of a job!"[1] That is why understanding and living by grace is so important for parents.

Maybe you've felt like screaming, "I can't do this! I'm not strong enough. I'll never be a good parent!" If so, I have great news for you: You are in the perfect place to benefit from God's grace, which is a limitless resource. God told the Apostle Paul, *"My grace is sufficient for you, for power is perfected in weakness."* In his weakness, Paul learned to depend on the power of Christ in him, and in the end, he concluded, *When I am weak, then I am strong* (2 Cor 12:9-10). That may seem counterintuitive, but because of what God does, it isn't. Embrace God's grace, and discover confidence, peace, assurance, joy, and hope on your parenting journey.

Grace: What It Teaches Us

God's grace is caricatured by some today as an antidote for the effects of sin: *Even if I don't obey God's commands or follow His will for my life, He'll make everything work out for me in the end.* That isn't grace; it's license. This is a fallacy that shallow Christianity has wrongly derived from Romans 8:28. People hone in on the first phrase: "And we know that God causes all things to work together for good," but brush over the two qualifying statements: "to those who love God, to those who are called according to His purpose." Grace does not cancel out the effects of sin. It teaches us the importance of avoiding sin.

In Titus 2:11-12, the Apostle Paul sums this up succinctly:

*For the grace of God has appeared, bringing salvation to all men,
instructing us to deny ungodliness and worldly desires and to live
sensibly, righteously and godly in the present age . . .*

God's grace, His goodness and unmerited favor, is exhibited
supremely in salvation, His gift of eternal life that is offered freely to
anyone and everyone who believes in Jesus Christ. There are no other
requirements to enter into a forever relationship with God. Jesus 'paid
it all' in His death on the cross: *Believe in the Lord Jesus and you will be
saved* (Acts 16.31).

But if God's grace means He loves us enough to give us eternal life,
it also means that He loves us enough to want us to escape from the
sin that once enslaved us. So, grace *instructs* us to "deny ungodliness
and worldly desires." To 'deny' is to repudiate or disown someone or
something. It is an intentional separation from sin. In a world that
has rejected God's plan for family stability—sex only in the context of
marriage between one man and one woman, for life (see Gen 2:24-25;
Matt 19:4-6; Rom 7:2-3; Eph 5:31), grace teaches us to embrace God's
way.

"But wait," someone will say, "what if I've already messed up? I'm
just discovering God in my life, and past sins have left deep scars. Is
there any hope for me?" Yes! My wife and I have eight children, but
we're still learning. Wherever you are in your journey of faith, God's
grace is sufficient to guide you through good times and bad.

Grace in Times of Trial

Facebook can get you down. All those pictures or videos of family
vacations, parents showing off their kids' accomplishments, or
husbands and wives enjoying a romantic night out at a nice restaurant.
You don't see many dirty diapers, children fighting with each other,
or disagreements between parents. Why? Because we like to present
ourselves as having it all together. We know this is a ruse, but as Janis
Ian sang in her haunting ballad *At Seventeen*, we 'play the game,' and

inevitably learn that 'dreams were all they gave for free.' In the real world, those dreams often turn into nightmares.

When reality strikes, and struggles come, Satan plants his seeds of doubt, and when these take root, they bring despair. *I can't do this . . . I'm weak.* The temptation to throw in the towel can be great. A husband is impotent, a wife has a miscarriage, a child is born with a handicap or dies from disease or in an accident. It wasn't anything you did; it's just the result of living in a fallen world, where the effects of sin cause sickness and death. Is grace sufficient in these situations?

I come from a large family: It seemed like my mother was always pregnant when I was growing up (she gave birth fourteen times, and I was the sixth-born). When I was in my early teens, my youngest brother, Dougie, just eighteen months old, was severely burned in a tragic accident. My father was a professor at Bible college, and students started a round-the-clock prayer vigil for my brother. For two weeks, his little body hovered between life and death, then he died.

Years later, I met someone who was a student at the Bible college during that time. He told me about the prayers for my brother, then recounted what happened the morning after his death. At breakfast that morning, students were informed that Dougie had died during the night. He had a class with my father at eight o'clock that morning. Students doubted my father would come, but showed up just in case. At eight o'clock sharp, my father entered and walked to the podium. The room fell silent. What could a father say at a time like this? My father began, "It is at times like this that you understand the sufficiency of God's grace." And he taught the class.

The trials and travails of parenting are tough. They tear at your soul and shake the foundations of your faith. They may make no sense to you right now. Only the assurance that God is gracious, that He will walk with us through the hardships of life, and that we can 'cast our cares on Him, because He cares for us' (1 Pet 5:7) will keep us going. But His grace *is* sufficient.

Don't wait for difficult times to nurture your faith in God's grace and goodness. When you are thriving in God's blessings and all seems to be well, *make time* to read His Word daily, and get alone for times of prayer. As the *Living Bible* paraphrases Ephesians 3:17, "May your roots go down deep into the soil of God's marvelous love." Do these in the good times, and in the hard times. God's grace will sustain you.

Grace to Face Your Failures

A greater challenge that confronts many parents is their own sin. Being born into God's family is the beginning of new life—eternal life. But that doesn't mean all our problems are over. Our enemy has a three-step plan, lust-sin-death (Jas 1:14-15); his goal is to burden our lives with sin. The Bible describes our struggle in terms of hand-to-hand combat (Eph 6:10-17), and none of us get out unscathed.

Satan prods and prompts us to sin; then, when we are reeling with the effects of sin, he 'piles on.' Scripture calls him "the accuser of the brethren" (Rev 12:10). His scheme is to tempt us to sin, then shout in our spirits, "What makes you think God loves you?! You're a failure, and that's all you'll ever be."

Marriages and families are under assault in modern society. Many carry scars of sexual abuse or premarital sexual relationships. About half of first marriages end in divorce, and often, this causes spouses to feel like 'damaged goods' for the rest of their lives. Others are trying to recover from gender confusion or sexual deviations that are overwhelming our culture.

This is where the transforming power of grace shines. Grace is an intensely personal thing. Its source is God, and His provision is suited for our unique needs. We release the power of grace when we recognize our need for it, and we recognize our need for it when we understand God's holiness, and admit our sinfulness. 'Coming clean' with God engages the power of His grace.

The Apostle Paul is one of the heroes of the New Testament, but he had a past. It was ugly. Near the end of his life, he wrote about it (1 Tim 1:12-17). He thanked God that even though he was once a blasphemer, a persecutor, and a violent man, 'the grace of our Lord was more than abundant' (14). When he assessed his own life, he was the worst sinner of all (15), but this just made him a greater trophy of God's grace. As he wrote in Romans 5:20, "where sin increased, grace abounded all the more."

Stepping out into a life of grace begins with an admission of need, recognizing our sin. If we try to pretend we don't have a struggle with sin, we're deceiving ourselves (1 John 1:8). If we try to justify our sin ("Everyone does it"), we are contradicting what God says (1 John 1:10). Instead of evading or excusing sin, confess it. 1 John 1:9 says, *If we confess our sins, He is faithful and righteous to forgive us our sins and to cleanse us from all unrighteousness.* When you become aware of your sin, immediately go to God: "Lord, I want to come clean with you. I agree with you that I have sinned. Thank you for forgiving my sin."

You've just connected with God's grace. No penance. No absolution. No acts of contrition. Just confess, and God forgives. He's not 'holding it over your head.' But He will reveal other sins you have overlooked in your life that need forgiveness, so you can confess them, too. That's grace.

A Home That Models Grace

A home is the perfect environment to nurture grace. But grace, like the most important things in life, is best *caught*, not *taught*. It begins with dad and mom, and becomes a natural expression of love in the lives of children. Once parents have embraced God's grace, they can 'show and tell' it to their children. You don't just 'tell' it; the two go hand-in-hand.

A husband models grace by *initiating* love for his wife. In Genesis 2:24, it is the *man* who leaves his father and mother, and cleaves to his wife. He enters into an exclusive and permanent covenant relationship of loyalty to and intimacy with her. His commitment is one of sacrificial love, "just as Christ also loved the church and gave Himself up for her" (Eph 5.25).

A wife models grace by *responsive* love for her husband. Her submission to his leadership in the marriage parallels the church's submission to Christ (Eph 5:23-24). The combination of love and submission is a virtual guarantee that God's grace will be modeled in a home. But let's explore this aspect of love a little further.

An old Christian chorus had these simple lyrics: *Love is something you do, love is something you do; Not only something that you feel, but it's real . . .* God's love for the world was demonstrated in Him sending

His Son, and this 'grace-gift' to the world involved *action*: Jesus died for my sin. A husband is commanded to love his wife "as Christ loved the church." What did Christ's love for the church entail? He gave his life for her. Someone has observed, "If you love your wife enough to die for her, you will love her enough to help with the dishes." That's true, but there's more.

A poignant scene in the movie *Fiddler on the Roof* takes place between Tevye and his wife Golde. Years before, they were the product of an arranged marriage, but the world has changed, and their daughters are marrying men for *love*. Sheldon Harnick's lyrics capture a deep longing in this exchange between husband and wife:

Tevye: "Golde . . . Do you love me?"

Golde: "Do I what?"

Tevye: "Do you love me?"

Golde: "Do I love you? With our daughters getting married, and this trouble in the town; you're upset, you're worn out, go inside, go lie down! Maybe it's indigestion."

Tevye: "Golde, I'm asking you a question. Do you love me?"

Golde: "You're a fool."

Tevye: "I know . . . but do you love me?"

Golde: "Do I love you? For twenty-five years I've washed your clothes, cooked your meals, cleaned your house, given you children, milked the cow; after twenty-five years, why talk about love right now?"

Tevye: "Golde, the first time I met you was on our wedding day. I was scared."

Golde: "I was shy."

Tevye: "I was nervous."

Golde: "So was I."

Tevye: "But my father and my mother said we'd learn to love each other, and now I'm asking, Golde, do you love me?"

Golde: "I'm your wife."

Tevye: "I know . . . but do you love me?"

Golde: "Do I love him? For twenty-five years I've lived with him,
        fought with him, starved with him. Twenty-five years my
        bed is his; if that's not love, what is?"

Tevye: "Then you love me?"

Golde: "I suppose I do."

Tevye: "And I suppose I love you, too."

What a sublime truth! While husbands and wives can show love
through things they do for each other, our hearts yearn for a deeper
experience. It's not just going through the motions. Golde washed and
cooked and cleaned for 25 years, but Tevye's question reached into her
heart.

According to Yale University psychologist Robert Sternberg, love
has three ingredients: Passion (romance), intimacy (affection), and
commitment (allegiance).[2] Passion may come and go, and commitment
will keep a marriage together, but intimacy is the 'heart' of love. In our
spiritual lives, grace brings us into a *relationship* with God by faith, but
the goal of grace is that we have *fellowship* with God. That's *intimacy*.
That's the pinnacle of Christian experience. Pursue intimacy in your
marriage, and you'll model God's grace.

Teaching Grace to Your Kids

Author Randy Alcorn writes that "parents' greatest heritage to pass
on to their children is the ability to perceive the multitude of God's
daily blessings and to respond with continual gratitude. We should be
'overflowing with thankfulness' (Col 2:7)."[3] Grace is at the center of all
God's blessings; being thankful is a natural response to that. So how
can we pass that lesson on to our children?

The best way to teach your children to have an 'attitude of gratitude'
is to cultivate that mindset yourself. From the early toddler years filled
with accidents, spilt milk, tantrums and endless laundry for mom, or
working long, stressful hours at the office and coming home to chaos
for dad, it's easy to slip into the 'martyr complex' that exhaustion and
discouragement often engender. When our commitment to family

becomes a labor of resentment rather than a labor of love, our home will inevitably lack peace and joy. But when we *intentionally* foster a grateful mindset ourselves, our children will learn to do the same, and the resulting healthier, more peaceful home environment will carry over into those complex teen years and help your children to avoid the pitfalls of entitlement and selfishness.

A child trained to thank God for blessings great and small will progressively understand the vastness of God's grace. Stopping, bowing heads, and giving thanks before a meal should not just be a ritual, but a heartfelt recognition of God's goodness. An environment of continual thanksgiving to God teaches some vital truths. Here are just a few.

First, *you didn't earn this.* The whole universe is God's creation. This beautiful world was made by Him for us. He created life, and that includes our lives; our parents conceived us, but only God can form life in the womb. Food doesn't come from a grocery store; God provides that. As the Bible puts it, *What do you have that you haven't received?* (1 Cor 4:7). Answer: Nothing.

Second, *you don't deserve this.* Grace is *unmerited favor*, getting what you *don't deserve.* Our 'entitlement culture' causes many growing up today to think that life 'owes them' something. Regularly giving thanks to God confronts this 'me-first' attitude by reminding us it's all from Him, and it's all because of grace.

Third, thankfulness engenders generosity: *The greatest joy comes through giving, not receiving.* As we cultivate an 'attitude of gratitude', the joy of giving, modeled completely by Christ on the cross, becomes part of our response. We have received grace, and we show grace. As Jesus said, "Freely you received, freely give" (Matt 10:8b). Winston Churchill was right: "We make a living by what we get. We make a life by what we give."

Encouraging the verbal expression of thanks to each other in the family setting is a great reminder to be truly thankful for all we have been given, and encourages us all to 'serve one another.' When this begins with mom and dad serving not only each other, but all members of the family, children mimic this grace gift of service, especially when it is showered with a generous helping of thankfulness.

A child will discern that acts of service are not earned, or even deserved, but are sourced in genuine kindness without the expectation of anything in return. This is a pure reflection of God's grace toward us.

As children grow and begin to see the contrast between their own grace-filled family and other families, they will see the destructive results of family members taking each other and their blessings for granted. Discontent and selfishness abound. Entitlement and self-righteousness become their anthem, and this echoes in our present culture. Our teens and young adults need an answer to the conflict and division they see in the world today. Grace is the antidote that will safeguard their hearts.

Grace and Identity

One area in which parenting with grace can have an enormous impact is the area of identity or self-esteem. Cultural forces are undermining biblical norms for our value, roles, and function as human beings. The result is mass confusion in children, and a seemingly fruitless and endless search for meaning and purpose. Grace is an antidote to this contemporary societal ill.

As noted above, a home is the perfect environment to nurture grace. But if parents have a faulty conception of God, this can result in a dysfunctional home life. A graceless home distorts God's character five ways. It caricatures God as 1) cruel and capricious, 2) demanding and unforgiving, 3) selective and unfair, 4) distant and unavailable, and 5) kind, but confused.[4] Satan loves to spread these pernicious lies about God, and a defective view of God's love and grace can lead to a damaged and deficient view of ourselves.

A core message of grace is this: You are valuable to God. You are important to God. You are loved by God. You are cared for by God. When children learn that their value is tied to their achievement, or that love is conditioned on their success, or become aware that they 'aren't as good' as other kids, inevitable failure results in shame, discouragement, and even depression.

My wife has counseled at a crisis pregnancy center for years. A common theme in those facing an uncertain future because of an unexpected and unplanned pregnancy is low self-esteem. They were looking for love in all the wrong places. They view themselves as worth little or nothing, and life holds no meaning or purpose. When the light of God's love and grace shines into their darkened hearts, it transforms their lives.

A grace-filled home gives a biblical view of God: He tirelessly seeks us, desires intimacy with us, is long-suffering and patient with us, and when we are weakest, He is strong. Godly parents will communicate this truth to their children often.

Grace and Tolerance

Earlier in this chapter we observed that grace is not an antidote for the effects of sin. A partner truth is that grace is not tolerance. Tolerance and grace are often thought to go hand-in-hand. You show grace to others by showing tolerance toward them. A dictionary definition of tolerance includes ideas like 'recognizing and respecting the beliefs and practices of others without sharing them,' and 'putting up with those you don't agree with.' But the concept of 'tolerance' has become more sinister.

In today's culture, 'tolerance' is being intolerantly demanded by various movements. It is no longer simply 'recognizing and respecting;' it has become 'endorsing and embracing.' Even remaining silent is unacceptable. Any variance from the culturally-approved view is deemed not just wrong, but evil. In the face of this cultural *intolerance*, how can we teach our children grace and *real* tolerance?

Tolerance must begin in the home. We teach our children to tolerate each other, not to demand tolerance for themselves. True tolerance understands that we are each imperfect, needing frequent forgiveness and grace—and this includes mom and dad. Once I punished one of my children, only to have my wife take me aside and inform me I got it wrong. I had to go to my child and ask forgiveness. When our children see us loving, forgiving, accepting, and showing grace to each other in the family, they learn tolerance.

The challenge parents face today is this: In a culture in which what God calls sin has become 'the new normal,' children need to learn that *grace does not mean tolerance of sin.* The Christian life is counter-culture. Sin is an offense to God, who has freely extended His grace to us. Loving and accepting a person who is in bondage to sin, without endorsing their sin, is how we show tolerance with grace. If a child grows up in a family where grace and forgiveness are consistently displayed, they learn that sinners are of great value to God, and not beyond the reach of His forgiveness and restoration. But demanding 'tolerance' for their sin is a rejection of God. When we sin, we need to confess it, and receive God's forgiving grace.

What if our sinning child is demanding 'tolerance' from us as parents? How do we show grace then? Remember that grace does not mean excusing sin; in fact, it means loving them enough to tell them that. Although their sin is an offense to God, they are still precious and valuable and loved, not only by us as their earthly parents, but by their heavenly Father as well. As Titus 2:12 says, it is the grace of God that 'instructs us to deny ungodliness and worldly desires and to live sensibly, righteously and godly in the present age.' It is our God and Savior, Jesus Christ against whom they are sinning, and it is He who gave Himself to redeem them and forgive them. That is the very essence of grace.

Grace and Discipline

Another area where many parents struggle is disciplining their children. While it may appear that grace and discipline are in conflict, and that grace might mean not giving discipline when it is warranted, the opposite is actually true. Parents who withhold discipline from their children don't teach them grace, but license.

Here our parental blueprint comes from our heavenly Father: *Those whom the Lord loves He disciplines, and He scourges every son whom He receives . . . for what son is there whom his father does not discipline?* (see Heb 12:5-11). Dave Anderson writes:

> We are in a family. God is our Father. A good father motivates his children positively and negatively. To motivate his child to do well, the father might offer certain rewards, even if it is just the reward of praise and approval. On the other hand, it helps the child to know there will be negative consequences should he or she choose to misbehave.[5]

In a day when parental discipline is frowned upon by many, parents need to heed what God says. The way God 'parented' His chosen people, the nation of Israel in the Old Testament, exhibits patience, grace and forgiveness, yet also discipline that was often harsh. But always present within His discipline was mercy for the children He loved. God did not act out of vindictive rage. When God lovingly rescued His children from bondage and planned a land flowing with milk and honey for them, they complained and rebelled, and worshipped the golden calf. Because of their rebellion, God kept them in the wilderness for 40 years; and a generation was denied entering the Promised Land. Yet even in this we see His grace and mercy. The wilderness was the 'classroom' where God taught His people to trust in Him. It prepared them for the challenges they would face in the conquest of the Promised Land. They learned to trust and obey. Loving parents show grace to their children by patiently disciplining them, and withholding freedom until the child has learned to trust and obey their earthly parents. At the same time, they will learn to trust and obey the Lord.

Speaking of God's discipline, the author of Hebrews ends his section on God's discipline with these words: *No discipline is enjoyable while it is happening—it's painful! But afterward there will be a peaceful harvest of right living for those who are trained in this way* (Heb 12:11, *New Living Translation*). My parents disciplined me often. I needed it. After receiving discipline, I never turned to my dad or mom and said, "Thanks for that fresh evidence of your love!" But I have often said that as an adult. I shudder to think where I would be today if they had withheld their discipline.

Keep the end goal in view. Your children may not express gratitude when you discipline them—in fact, they may express something very different. But loving discipline is part and parcel of parenting with grace.

Grace and Truth in a Post-Modern World

Without truth, there is no need for grace. Without grace, there is no need for truth. To put that positively, "We should never approach truth except in a spirit of grace, or grace except in a spirit of truth."[6]

How do you do that, in a post-modern world where 'truth' has become relative?

In 1960, at the height of the post-World War II baby boom, there was one dominant family form. 73% of children lived in a family with two married parents in their first marriage. By 1980, that number had slipped to 61%, and today, less than half (46%) are. The decline of the "traditional" family has been matched by an increase in the number of children living in homes with single or cohabiting parents.[7] How do parents in non-traditional families communicate grace and truth to their children?

Parents today are discovering that they need to be educated in the ways our world is influencing the thinking of our teen and young adult children. No longer do we have a culture that mirrors the values we teach our children at home; instead, we hear loud, angry voices that are in direct opposition to them.

Let's face it: Unless we live in a bubble and keep our children completely isolated from the surrounding culture, we will have to face many tough issues with them. The best way to do this is for us to *intentionally* ground them in their faith, so they are able to withstand the influence of peers, teachers, YouTubers, bloggers, and even some churches and Christian groups. Parents can be ready for these conversations, expressing love, support, and grace.

Importantly, we can set the stage and create an atmosphere in which these conversations can take place. Too often, the norm for teens today is to come home from school, retreat to their bedroom, and watch YouTubers or video-gamers for hours on end. We would be foolish to believe that this does not influence their thinking and the formation of their worldview.

The adolescent Christian today encounters a barrage of issues which directly challenge biblical faith: Gender identity, Critical Race Theory, sexual confusion, guilt, abuse, bullying, neglect or abandonment, hopelessness, rage, and fear. Those who stray from 'correct' views will face the 'cancel culture' which pressures them to be silent, and even decries them as being evil. This is a form of tribalism where a line is drawn in the sand and they are forced to take a side. This often leads to depression and suicide—with suicide now the second leading cause of death among those aged 15-24. Many Christians fall away from the faith during their college years.

How do we encourage our teens to hold fast to their faith in this hostile climate? How do we safeguard their hearts and help them stay strong? As noted above, affirming their value, with an identity based in grace, is critical. This happens in a grace-filled home. A secure, committed, loving family life is an atmosphere in which a child can thrive. They know *who* they are, and their family is their identity. That is where they belong. Conversely, where a household consists of mom and the boy-friend, the children lack not only stability, but security. They do not have the same sense of belonging in this fractured family unit and their identity is shaky.

As a child grows in a well-established family unit, where mom and dad serve one another in love and grace, they observe what Jesus' love is like. Make this the number one goal for your family. The more the love of Christ is displayed in the home, the more a child identifies with that love as they begin to understand who they are in Christ. *This becomes their identity.* By the time they reach their teen years, where their faith will be challenged, knowing who they are in Christ will safeguard them from other identity crises that battle for their souls.

In order for our children to stand firm in their faith 'not tossed to and fro by the waves and carried about by every wind of doctrine' (Eph 4.14), parents need to be grounded *themselves* in the Truth of God's Word, and then intentionally teach it to their children. Sadly, many churches and religious institutions no longer hold to the absolute Truth of Scripture, with devastating results. If the Bible is not trusted as 'Absolute Truth,' we are each left to determine what is 'truth' for us, what is morally right, what is sin—in essence, we become our own god.

Into this vacuum of truth, a godly Christian parent injects truth in a spirit of grace, and grace in a spirit of truth. I know of no better way to achieve this than through family devotions, especially when children are young and their lives are home-centered. As they approach the adolescent years, make personal time to come alongside them and talk about difficult issues. Growing up in a home with regular times of Bible reading and prayer will ground children in biblical truth and a recognition of God's grace. Scripture tells us that "the Light shines in the darkness." This Light is the Living Word, Jesus, who is "full of grace and truth" (John 1:5, 14). As we nurture children in the love and truth of Jesus, and they see us standing firm in the faith, they will have the courage to shine the Light that the darkness can never overcome.

When a child leaves the nest to begin a new journey in life, they will face challenges to their faith. Knowing their family is praying for them, and knowing they can talk freely about any fears or confusion they encounter, will be a great source of confidence for them as they step into adulthood.

Having the Grace to Let Go

In a world that seems to daily descend ever deeper into evil, parents may feel an urge to hold tightly to their children. It's natural for us to want to protect them from sin and its influence. But in a grace-filled home, parents know that God's grace extends beyond their physical control. The 'grace to let go' is how we exhibit our faith in His goodness; we give our children back to the Lord who gave them to us, entrusting them to Him to mature their faith.

Parents teach truth, model grace, and love unconditionally, but it is God who tests and 'proves' our children's faith. His purifying and refining process is necessary for them to go on to spiritual maturity. As James 1:3-4 says, "the testing of your faith produces endurance. And let endurance have its perfect result, so that you may be perfect and complete, lacking in nothing." Isn't that the goal of every Christian parent? We demonstrate faith in our gracious God by having the grace to let go and trust Him to complete the good work that He has started.

God gave marriage as a picture of His undying love for us. He is our Heavenly Bridegroom and we, the church, are His bride. Marriage is sacred, as it is God's gift to mankind to reflect His love. In the same way, He gave us family, and in our families, we model God's grace as we learn to serve one another with a heart of gratitude for the One who loves us most of all.

---

[1] Howard Hendricks, *Heaven Help the Home* (Wheaton, Ill.: Victor Books, 1973), 135.

[2] Les Parrott III and Leslie Parrott, *Saving Your Marriage Before It Starts: Seven Questions to Ask Before (and After) You Marry* (Grand Rapids: Zondervan Publishing House, 1995), 33-35.

[3] Randy Alcorn, *The Grace and Truth Paradox* (Sisters, Oregon: Multnomah Publishers, 2003), 46.

[4] Sandra D. Wilson, *Released from Shame: Moving Beyond the Pain of the Past*, rev. ed. (Downers Grove, IL: IVP Books, 2002), 141-156.

[5] Dave Anderson, *Saving the Saved: An Exposition of 1 Peter* (Grace Theology Press, 2020), 72.

[6] Randy Alcorn, *The Grace and Truth Paradox*, 16.

[7] "The American Family Today," *Pew Research Center: Social and Demographic Trends*, December 17, 2015, https://www.pewsocialtrends.org/2015/12/17/1-the-american-family-today/, accessed August 26, 2020.

Chapter 4

Grace and Vocation

Mark Rae, M.Div.

Introduction

Work is what consumes the majority of our weekly waking hours. Work for many is what gives meaning to our lives. Work is that thing that can either excite us or drain us. Work is what we use to accomplish the tasks that have been set before us. Many go to school and get degrees in specific arenas of work in order to be able to do the work better. Many fall into various types of work. Many purpose to focus on specific venues of work, and many find themselves in a work field that they wonder, "How did I get here?" But have we ever stopped to think about our work in the proper Biblical perspective? That our work is a gift of grace from God? The Bible has a tremendous amount to say about our work, and not just the work of ministry. Dating all the way back to the Garden of Eden and the first people—Adam and Eve—work, then and now, was given as a gift of grace to us from God Himself. Throughout the Scriptures, from the Old Testament to the New Testament, work is spoken about as a gift of grace from God to His creation.

In order to better understand this, we must first take a quick look at the word grace. Though this word has multiple meanings depending on the context and how it is being used, in this instance we are looking at the word grace in the context of something that is given to another. In this case, grace is defined by the phrase "*unmerited favor*" meaning that whatever the gift is that we are given, we have not earned it, nor purchased it, nor even deserved it. It is a favor given that is unmerited—not given on the basis of merit. As we will see going all the way back to the Garden in Genesis, God, out of His gracious love for us, graced us with work. We are going to start in the Garden and trace some of the major passages of Scripture that deal with work and see them as the gracious gifts of God to us, even today. With this perspective of grace and work, the prayer is that we will see our work in a different and blessed way which can transform how we view the place where we spend the majority of our time and energy.

The Scriptural Basis of Grace at Work

In order to understand how God views your work, we start at the beginning with the Genesis account and the first Covenant Promise that God made with Adam. Notice that prior to this, the Trinity was at work in creating the heavens and the earth. Work was already being established as the way of life complete with a period of rest, rejoicing, and gratefulness mixed in.

In Genesis 1:26-28 we read, *"Then God said, "Let Us make man in Our image, according to Our likeness; let them have dominion over the fish of the sea, over the birds of the air, and over the cattle, over all the earth and over every creeping thing that creeps on the earth." So God created man in His own image; in the image of God He created him; male and female He created them. Then God blessed them, and God said to them, "Be fruitful and multiply; fill the earth and subdue it; have dominion over the fish of the sea, over the birds of the air, and over every living thing that moves on the earth."*

God creates man and woman, and simply because they are a creation of God, He *gives them* dominion or graces them with the responsibility of caring for the fish and the birds and the cattle and the creeping things. God gives Adam and Eve the gift of overseeing His creation and neither Adam nor Eve had done anything to earn that gift. That is grace—unmerited favor.

After creating them and blessing them, God then gives them their work. That privilege of working with God in His garden is seen in the little Hebrew word that is translated "fruitful." God tells Man to be fruitful and multiply. That Hebrew word, "*Parah*," means to bear fruit but we often attach it to the word 'multiply' and take it to mean 'have children.' Instead, it can also be translated this way—"be productive." In other words, God's mandate to Adam and Eve was to be productive— go produce by taking dominion and subduing creation on behalf of God. Go bear fruit through your tending and keeping and God's blessing will be upon you.

Genesis 2:15 sheds more light on this point when we read, *"Then the Lord God took the man and put him in the garden of Eden to tend and keep it."* Here we see the expansion of the word 'parah' when the words "tend" and "keep" are added to it. We now understand that Man's work was to tend and keep God's Garden and to enjoy it because man was working alongside God as His creation in His creation. What an undeserved honor and a privilege.

I can remember when my two boys were growing up and the time came for them to learn how to take care of our lawn by mowing, edging, and sweeping. I had always taken great care to keep my yard looking well-cared-for, so I took the time and the effort to teach them and to show them how to *tend and keep* the yard. I am certain that they did not see this as a privilege. However, after taking time to make sure they knew what to do, I turned over the responsibility of the yard to them. This was not easy to do because they did not always tend to the yard in the manner in which I had taught them, but they did a very good job. Now look at what God did; He turned over the tending and caring for His garden—His creation— to Adam and Eve. This was an incredible gift of grace because they had not earned this privilege, and yet God graced the garden to them.

We know what happened—The Fall, and yet in Genesis 3:17-19, where we see the effects of The Fall on Adam in the curse for his sin, we still see God's gracious hand on him.

Then to Adam He said,

"Because you have heeded the voice of your wife, and have eaten
from the tree of which I commanded you, saying, 'You shall not
eat of it':

"Cursed is the ground for your sake;

In toil you shall eat of it

All the days of your life.

Both thorns and thistles it shall bring forth for you,

And you shall eat the herb of the field.

In the sweat of your face you shall eat bread

Till you return to the ground,

For out of it you were taken;

For dust you are,

And to dust you shall return."

Though both Adam and Eve deserved death for their sin, God
instead still allows Adam to tend the garden and work the land, but
it will not be easy. Though it will produce thorns and thistles, they
will still be able to eat from their labors. Take note that the gift of
work was introduced before the Fall and the entrance of sin. Work is
not a punishment for sin and never was intended to be though it was
affected by sin. Work was given by God to be a blessing and part of
the Covenant promise that God made with Adam—that His creation
would be a blessing to man and that man would be gifted the privilege
of caring for it.

As we move forward in our Old Testament search, we next find
work included in the Ten Commandment in Exodus 20:8-11.

"Remember the Sabbath day, to keep it holy. Six days you shall
labor and do all your work, but the seventh day is the Sabbath of
the Lord your God. In it you shall do no work: you, nor your son,

nor your daughter, nor your male servant, nor your female servant, nor your cattle, nor your stranger who is within your gates. For in six days the Lord made the heavens and the earth, the sea, and all that is in them, and rested the seventh day. Therefore, the Lord blessed the Sabbath day and hallowed it."

God says to the nation that they should work for six days, but on the seventh they should rest. God's original design for work was that humans would spend their lives in productive activity with regular breaks for leisure, and rest, and to celebrate God's blessings. The Hebrew word for work or labor, "avodah," can also be translated into "service," meaning that our work is our service unto the Lord, but it can also have the meaning of worship. So, when we put those three words together, we get this picture of work—our work is our service to God, and it is also our worship to God. Did you ever stop to think about your work as your service and worship to God? This puts a whole new spin on our work and God's view of it.

Our next passage on work comes in the Book of Ecclesiastes and here we get perhaps one of the best views on the graciousness of God in the gift of our work. In Ecclesiastes 2:24-25 we read that *"Nothing is better for a man than that he should eat and drink, and that his soul should enjoy good in his labor. This also, I saw, was from the hand of God. For who can eat, or who can have enjoyment, more than I?"*

This passage should make us sit up and pay close attention because what we find here is the superlative phrase, *nothing is better*. After the Fall and the curse, we still find that nothing is better for a man than that he should enjoy good in his labor. What a ringing endorsement for work! Enjoying good from our labor is the best thing. We are to find enjoyment in our work. Why? Because our work is from the very hand of a good God and good work from the very hand of a good God is good for the soul. This is the way God designed it and the way we were meant to engage in it. The gift of grace which is our work was meant to be understood and enjoyed as the gift from a gracious and good God.

When we move to the New Testament passages, we see a very interesting pattern emerge. Work was a part of the everyday life of the Disciples and Jesus. In fact, Jesus was a worker who spent the first thirty years of his life as a "tecton;" literally a stonemason in the Greek. Jesus worked with wood and stone as He built with His hands. Paul was a tentmaker; Peter was a fisherman as were several other Disciples; and Matthew was a tax collector. However, notice what Jesus says about work in John 5:17:

> But Jesus answered them, *"My Father has been working until now, and I have been working."*

Jesus states that both He and God are workers. We know that they worked together at creation and here in the mundane things of life, we see Jesus working. Perhaps we could be so bold as to state that if both Jesus and God were workers, then shouldn't we be workers as well? Shouldn't we see our work as the gift of grace that it is from the hand of a good God? They set the example for us in work and they set the example for us in other areas as well. They set the example in how to love another, in how to serve another, in how to care for another, in how to sacrifice for another, and in how to extend grace to others.

Our final two passages come from the Apostle Paul. In Ephesians 2:10 Paul writes, *"For we are His workmanship, created in Christ Jesus for good works, which God prepared beforehand that we should walk in them."*

Notice several things: first, we are described as the workmanship, the very handiwork, of God created through the person of Christ. Did you ever consider yourself to be the very handiwork of God through Christ? You had nothing to do with that—that is grace. Second, you were created for good works. Think about that for a moment— you were created to do good works—what a truth and a wonderful purpose statement for your life. Do you think of your work as your place of service to Christ—the place to do good works? He not only gives you the work, but He gives you the place to serve Him though your work. What this means is that the term "full-time ministry" really refers to anyone who works. This is the place where they serve Christ, and it is the place where their arena of service exists. The pastor serves Christ in the church by grace, the missionary serves Christ on the mission field by grace, the worker serves Christ where they work by grace. All who work are in service to Christ where we work by His grace. Third, God has already prepared the good works for you to walk in. The whole world is a theater of God's glory and working in the world has value to God because it has been graced by God. We are called to service and though the arena of service can change, the calling to serve remains the same. It is a calling made possible because of grace. We did nothing to earn it or deserve it. You are a good work, the work that you do is a good work, the good works that come from your work are good works, and the place where you work is a place to serve Christ. These are all yours by grace.

Paul finally brings the point of service and work and grace home in this little passage written to the church at Colossae. In Colossians 3:23-24, he writes to slaves who have masters and states, *"And whatever you do, do it heartily, as to the Lord and not to men, knowing that from the Lord you will receive the reward of the inheritance; for you serve the Lord Christ."*

Whom do we serve when we work? We serve the Lord and not men, and there is a reward awaiting us for this faithful service. Do we deserve that reward? No, not on our own merit but because we serve the Lord Christ. It is an act of grace on His part to give that reward. To add emphasis, Paul states again whom we serve—WE SERVE THE LORD CHRIST! We are servants of Christ and the place where we spend the majority of our waking hours—our work—is the place where we are called to serve Him and to serve Him faithfully and with excellence. He has given us this work by grace, and it is time that we see our work as the gift of grace that it is from a good and gracious God and from his Son, Jesus Christ.

The Practical Basis of Grace at Work

Why work? A great question, and one that needs to be answered for every individual who works or is coming to the age where they will work. We have seen in this walk through the Scriptures that the grace of God was extended to us by giving us the gift of work. However, there are also very practical applications of this gift of work that are evident in the Scriptures as well. God saw to it that through our work, the reality of His grace would take care of the very practical daily needs that we would encounter. Listed below are a collection of those very practical applications where we see the grace of God extends to us daily in the everyday situations of life. He meets us there and graces us through our work to be able to extend that grace to others as it has been extended to us.

Initially we see that through our work, we have the opportunity to care for ourselves. This is seen when Paul writes in 2 Thessalonians 3:10-12, *"For even when we were with you, we commanded you this: If anyone will not work, neither shall he eat. For we hear that there are some who walk among you in a disorderly manner, not working at all, but are busybodies. Now those who are such we command and exhort through our Lord Jesus Christ that they work in quietness and eat their own bread."*

What Paul is explaining is the very real fact that those who do not work, do not eat. When we pray, give us this day our daily bread, what we acknowledge is that our daily bread comes from God and that we are dependent upon Him to supply that bread. One significant way that He supplies that is through the gift of our work. Therefore when we exercise that gift, we get the blessing of being able to eat and survive. We can take care of ourselves through our work.

Paul now turns that gift outward when he writes in 1 Timothy 5:8 that we can care for our families. He says, *"But if anyone does not provide for his own, and especially for those of his household, he has denied the faith and is worse than an unbeliever."*

God specifically saw the need for families to be cared for and He gifted us with work in order to ensure that our families had what they needed. Notice how seriously Paul takes this gift of grace in exhorting Christians to provide for their families—he states that one who does not provide for his household has denied the faith and is worse than an unbeliever. The culture of the day was that family members have a duty to care for one another and even the world of unbelievers does this. Therefore, if a Christian does not work and provide for his family, he has gone against the teaching of his faith and is worse than the unbeliever because even the unbeliever cares for his family. The example that was set for us was Christ Himself who, while He hung on the cross, called upon John to care for His mother,

Mary. The gift of grace in our work should see that grace extend to others.

Paul shows this truth even more so when he states in Ephesians 4:28, *"Let him who stole steal no longer, but rather let him labor, working with his hands what is good, that he may have something to give him who has need."*

We see here a direct connection between our work and our generosity to others. Paul exhorts those in the church to work with their hands to a good end—that being the ability to give out of the abundance of that work to those who have need. Since we have been graced with work, we are to grace others who have need. Paul continues this message in his letter to the Corinthian church when he states in 2 Corinthians 8:13-15,

> *For I do not mean that others should be eased and you burdened; but by an equality, that now at this time your abundance may supply their lack, that their abundance also may supply your lack—that there may be equality. As it is written, "He who gathered much had nothing left over, and he who gathered little had no lack."*

This is the blessing of work—that out of the overflow of what good work brings, other's needs can be met. When there is no overflow from your work, others can help meet your needs. Gracious work is the means in the church for assisting those in need. God also saw to it that we should get the benefit of caring for those in need. Throughout the Old and New Testaments, God's love for the unfortunate is well documented. He cares for the widows, the orphans, and the poor. He desires us to do so as well. Our work is an avenue through which we can bless others as God has blessed us.

Paul now moves on to a mission from work that is close to his heart—the church. Through our work, we can care for the church and the ministry that emanates from the body of Christ. In 1 Thessalonians 2:9, Paul writes, *"For you remember, brethren, our labor and toil; for laboring night and day, that we might not be a burden to any of you, we preached to you the gospel of God."*

Here Paul makes the case that his toil and labor was for the sake of the gospel—the work of the church—to share the good news of Jesus Christ. Work provides a way for us to support the work of God in the world though the church. Paul shares that his desire was not to be a burden to the church but to share the gospel, thus expanding the reach of the church.

We also see in his letter to the church at Philippi where he thanks them for their continued support of his work on behalf of the gospel. He shares this in Philippians 4:10-20, *"But I rejoiced in the Lord greatly that now at last your care for me has flourished again; though you surely did care, but you lacked opportunity. Not that I speak in regard to need, for I have learned in whatever state I am, to be content: I know how to be abased, and I know how to abound. Everywhere and in all things I have learned both to be full and to be hungry, both to abound and to suffer need. I can do all things through Christ who strengthens me.*

Nevertheless, you have done well that you shared in my distress. Now you Philippians know also that in the beginning of the gospel, when I departed from Macedonia, no church shared with me concerning giving and receiving but you only. For even in Thessalonica you sent aid once and again for my necessities. Not that I seek the gift, but I seek the fruit that abounds to your account. Indeed, I have all and abound. I am full, having received from Epaphroditus the things sent from you, a sweet-smelling aroma, an acceptable sacrifice, well pleasing to God. And my God shall supply all your need according to His riches in glory by Christ Jesus. Now to our God and Father be glory forever and ever. Amen."

Paul concludes his letter to this church with a thank you for their financial and spiritual support for him while he is in prison. Notice that he states in his rejoicing that the care that they previously shared with him has not returned, and that he is sure that they wanted to continue but could not for some reason. Now that they have, he is greatly encouraged because this church shared not only in his financial well-being but also in his emotional distress from his imprisonment. They have supported him from the beginning of the church, and he mentions several instances where their support was of great help in supplying his necessities. But perhaps the most telling thing about the gift of grace that flows from our work to others is the blessing that it is to us. This is how God's economy works. He graces us, we grace others, and we share the blessings of that grace. Paul says that he was not so much concerned about their gift but was more concerned about the fruit (reward) that would be credited to their account. His praise was that their sacrificial gift would be a sweet-smelling aroma, pleasing to God. What a beautiful way to think about the sharing of grace that comes out of the abundance of our work, which was a good gift of grace from God. Our work allows us the opportunity to support the work of the church in our communities and around the world. The body of Christ supports the work of the body of Christ. That is grace.

Finally, Paul shares that our work can be the place where we actually have the opportunity to share our faith by living it out in front of our co-workers on the job. In 1 Thessalonians 4:11-12 Paul writes, "*That you also aspire to lead a quiet life, to mind your own business, and to work with your own hands, as we commanded you, that you may walk properly toward those who are outside, and that you may lack nothing.*"

Paul admonishes the people of the church at Thessalonica to work with their hands—do physical labor—and through that to be able to walk properly toward those who are not believers. In other words, do your work well and with integrity so that the people who work alongside of you would see how the believers of the church worked and how they lived, and in doing so would see their faith in Christ. Notice also that the additional blessing of lacking nothing is also at play here. They can show the love of Christ to those they work with and lack nothing because of their work. What an incredible two-fold blessing through the gift of their work. God uses the gift of our work to care for ourselves, care for our families, care for others who are less fortunate, care for the work of the church, and care about sharing our faith in Christ.

The Value of Your Work to God

We have now taken a fairly in-depth look at the Biblical basis for work in our lives and have seen the very hand of God blessing us and gracing us with not only the practical value of our work, but also the fundamental principle of work—that God values what we do. Our work has both an Instrumental value and an Intrinsic value. The Instrumental value of our work means that through our work, we have the opportunity to accomplish another deeper goal. We have seen the Instrumental value of our work in those practical applications of caring for ourselves, our families, others, the work of the church, and providing a place to share our faith with our friends and coworkers.

Does our work then have value in and of itself? Does the work that we do actually have value to God? The answer is—absolutely! Our work has Intrinsic value in that the work itself is valuable to God, meaning that through our occupations we actually are accomplishing God's work in His creation. We are doing the work that God desires us to do in order to fulfill the mandate to tend and care for His creation. Therefore, the work itself is an intrinsically good thing because God ordained it and when we do the work with excellence, we are reflecting God and serving Him through that work.

Our work—your work—was ordained before the entrance of sin; was commanded in the original Adamic Covenant, the covenant made between God and Adam; is not a necessary evil but is a gift with inherent dignity; is done in partnership with God; is a reflection of God and Christ, as they were both workers; and because it was patterned after God in creation, is a pattern for all time. What a magnificent gift of grace!

All valid work is sacred to God and a place for sacred service to Him. As Paul tells us in Colossians 3:23-24, we serve Christ by doing our work faithfully and with excellence. Seeing work from both the Instrumental value and the Intrinsic value can radically change how we view our work. After all, if it was important enough to God to grace us with it, then it should be important enough to us to do it with integrity, excellence, and joy. When we see our work as a gift from the hand of God, we begin to see it in its proper perspective—that all of us are in full-time ministry because we are in service to the Lord through our work. In this respect, the term full-time ministry refers to one's attitude toward service rather than one's arena of service. To put a fine point to it, we serve Christ full-time through our work by the value of the work itself, by the way we do the work, and by the platform the work gives us to make Christ known.

Practical Advice to the Pastor

This new perspective on work has tremendous application for the pastor in viewing his congregation, and for the church member. To the pastor / shepherd, it will serve him or her well to remember that on Sunday, the day when most interaction with the flock occurs, the congregation comes to the church looking for spiritual and biblical answers to their weekly and sometimes daily issues. They live in the working world weekly for forty, fifty, sixty, or seventy hours and on Sunday, the issues at work do not magically disappear for the one to two hours that they are in the care of the pastors. If the pastor / shepherd does not know the sheep; what they do, and what their issues are, or is not understanding of what their work world is like, then he or she cannot speak to their issues and will not be relevant to them nor will the Word of God be relevant to them.

Many pastors go straight from college, to seminary, to the church, and have experienced the working world minimally, where the vast majority of their church body lives. Nor do they take the time to experience and understand the working world of their congregations— where and how they live daily. The pastor needs to get to know the church body in their environment and not the other way around.

I spent twenty plus years in the world of sales and marketing and in that time, I was a regular attender at church and knew the staff of different churches fairly well. In that time of twenty plus years, I never once had a pastor meet me at my place of work or talk to me anyplace other than the church. Now all of these pastors were good spiritual people, and I knew that they cared about me, but they had no idea about what my world was like because they never visited me in my world. When I became a pastor, I made sure that I met people where it was convenient to them. I met them at their offices, at coffee shops, or in their homes. Rarely did I meet them at the church, and when I did, it was primarily to have privacy for counseling. I do not share this to put myself on a pedestal, but simply to say that I best shepherded the members of the church when I got to know them where they lived and where they spent the majority of their time. I was much better prepared to speak from the Scriptures about their issues because I knew their issues, having spent time with them away from the confines of the church.

When you, as a pastor / shepherd, get to know your congregants through their work, you will be better able to shepherd them and to extend God's grace to them. They want you to know them and to know and understand their work. They want their work to matter and you can help them see the value of their work to God by making their work valuable to you beyond supporting the church and its ministry. God has called them to serve Him through their work and when you see that and affirm that in their lives, you affirm their value to them, and you affirm them to God—you extend God's grace to them.

Practical Advice to Mr. or Mrs. Joe Pew

In case you have not registered this truth by this time, here it is again—your work is valuable to God and so are you. You are abundantly graced by Him and your work is the place where you have been called to serve the Lord. It is time to see it that way and to treat your work as the gift of grace from God that it is. This is the place God has called you to serve Him because He needs you to serve Him here (not that God actually needs anyone or anything) but by His grace, He gives us the privilege of working with Him. We are in partnership with God to care for and tend to His creation. Our work is gifted by Him to us to do just that.

Your work is also the place God uses to refine you and to work out your spiritual formation because it is at work that you will find some of the biggest challenges in relationships, and challenges to morals and ethics. Since this is where you spend most of your weekly time and effort, it is also where God spends His time and effort with you, training you, and molding you, and shaping you into the image of Christ, who, by the way, was and is a worker.

The whole world is a showplace of God's glory and working in His world has value to Him and to us. When we do it with integrity and excellence, we serve Him well and put Him on display for the world to see. In doing that, we fulfill the mandate that was given all the way back in Genesis—to tend and keep His garden on His behalf and to make Him known in His creation.

Conclusion

Though we have barely scratched the surface on this topic, there are many who have studied and developed the theological basis for this, and there are a number of great resources listed at the end of this chapter that are recommended to study this further. Thanks to Dr. Scott Rae for the many hours of conversation as well as his teaching and writing on this important subject that have influenced me and the things that I share and teach.

Now, as a final exclamation point to the issue of grace and work, let's return to the Old Testament and to the prophet Isaiah. In Isaiah 2:4, we read,

> "He shall judge between the nations,
> And rebuke many people;
> They shall beat their swords into plowshares,
> And their spears into pruning hooks;
> Nation shall not lift up sword against nation,
> Neither shall they learn war anymore."

In the Kingdom, swords will be beaten into plowshares and spears will be beaten into pruning hooks. The prophet tells us that work will still be here because the instruments of war will be beaten into implements of work. There will still be productive work as part of the program of God after Christ returns. Work is a gift of grace from God to us and it is the place where we get the privilege of partnering with Him in pursuit of the mandate to tend His Garden. It is the place where He partners with us to shape us, through the power of His Spirit, into the image of His Son. As Ecclesiastes 2:24-25 tell us, "Nothing is better for a man than that he should eat and drink, and that his soul should enjoy good in his labor. This also, I saw, was from the hand of God. For who can eat, or who can have enjoyment, more than I?"

Our work is a gift of grace from the hand of God and it was created to be the place where God enters in with us into His creation and fulfills much of what He wants to do in us and in the world. Thanks be to God for our work—this incredible gift of grace.

Bibliography

Nelson, Tom. *Work Matters: Connecting Sunday Worship to Monday Work*. Wheaton, Illinois: Crossway, 2011.

Rae, Scott B. and Kenman L. Wong. *Business for the Common Good*. Downers Grove, Illinois: InterVarsity Press, 2011.

Stevens, R. Paul. *Work Matters: Lessons from Scripture*. Grand Rapids Michigan: Wm. B. Eerdmans Publishing Co. 2012.

Van Duzer, Jeff. *Why Business Matters to God: (And Still Needs to be Fixed)*. Downers Grove, Illinois: InterVarsity Press, 2010.

Chapter 5

A Grace that Mitigates . . .

Dr. Mark Haywood

Therefore, whatever you want men to do to you, do also to them,
for this is the Law and the Prophets.

Matthew 7:12

My Dad, Tom H. Haywood, was raised in the segregated State of Mississippi. As you could imagine, he was confronted by state-sponsored racism on a daily basis and such other indignities a Black person was destined to encounter in the midst of the Jim Crow South. These included being precluded from reserving a room at certain hotels, not permitted to dine at certain eateries (or having to receive your food at the backdoor or a side window), prevented from exercising one's right to vote in our democratic society (because of poll taxes, literacy tests, or guessing how many jelly beans are contained in a jar), challenged by legislative gerrymandering and "redlining" of certain neighborhoods to deny essential government goods and services, faced with housing discrimination (which destined one to a particular locale, and exposed to separate but unequal education), dealt with banks that would not extend loans based on one's zip code, poor medical treatment and care, and yes, confronted by the lynching and murder of innocent people. This list is not meant to be exhaustive but illustrative of the draconian daily life experienced in Mississippi that evidenced a type of dystopia for those who were the targets of racism and Jim Crow laws. In addition, the description of the life and times of Blacks during earlier times in the American South should not be viewed as censoriousness on the part of this author (as God will judge those practices) but simply chronicling the historical testimonies from the many folks who suffered through those times and the courageous historians willing to speak the truth.

Notwithstanding the above, my Dad trusted Christ at the tender age of twelve. As a result of Christ regenerating his heart, he believed the Bible is God's word, it is true, and that he needed to live in accordance with its truths. Thus, Dad grew up not only believing in Christian values but also doing his best to practice them. He immediately began to implement and incorporate spiritual disciplines into his daily routine. Now, fast forward to his adulthood and family life, Dad would regularly quote the above epigram, Matt 7:12, around our home. In fact, it was almost a daily occurrence. Moreover, the Scripture he cited most often is known as the "golden rule," and he quoted Prov 3:5-6, "Trust in the Lord with all your heart, And lean not on your own understanding; In all your ways acknowledge Him, And He shall direct your paths." Dad had committed these Scriptures to memory, and this was his methodology of inculcating into all seven of his children the importance of extending "grace" to everyone we might encounter during our earthly journey. Dad's goal was to help us avoid hubris and possess a healthy and biblical view of ourselves and others. Moreover, he believed that people were personally responsible for offering such grace to everyone regardless of racial and/or ethnic background. Further, grace was at the very core of Dad's spiritual journey and a key component of his approach to relationships, regardless of one's ethnicity.

During my lifetime, I enjoyed a front-row seat watching our Dad win people over with this simple yet biblical approach, which leads us to the discussion at hand. My purpose herein is to focus on grace and how it can and should impact our relationships among the various ethnic groups. To realize this goal, I will define key terms related to grace and racism, demonstrate various manifestations of racism and its ubiquitous nature (here, this chapter will not dedicate time towards establishing the existence of racism as it is axiomatic), as well as offer biblical approaches to sharing grace. Moreover, it is the contention of this chapter that racism is a sin and as long as sin exists, so too will racism. Despite our inability to eradicate it, we can mitigate it if church ministries, as well as individual believers assume a pugilistic stance against this plague on our society whether we engender the fortitude to admit its presence or not!

One must note that this chapter is not designed to indict, blame, or embarrass anyone on this very difficult subject. On the other hand, one of the objectives of this chapter is to expose areas of racism, prejudice, discrimination (and the like), so that believers who aim to live holy and please God might be aware and discover opportunities to insert grace when dealing with other ethnicities and avoid even unconscious biases.

Grace is one of the keys to combating the invidious and insidious nature of racism and the repugnant consequences of it. Nevertheless, we must first define grace, racism, and other key terms related to this subject matter. That being said, grace is bestowing favor upon a person who does not deserve it, did not earn it, and is offered without strings attached (that is, free). The term grace occurs approximately 148 times in our English Bible and may be found in both the Old and New Testaments (with its use in the New Testament about 128 times), carrying the sense that it is "unmerited favor." The Old Testament deploys a couple of diverse words that denote grace, but the New Testament word for grace is translated as "charis." One lexicon describes grace as, "*a beneficent disposition toward someone, favor, grace, gracious care/help, goodwill; practical application of goodwill, (a sign of) favor, gracious deed/gift, benefaction; exceptional effect produced by generosity, favor.*"[1] Embedded in each facet of this term, "grace" is the idea of undeserved favor, goodwill, and benevolence extended from God to humanity and from humanity to his fellow-citizenry. In addition, grace is so important to relationships among ethnic groups because it is a uniquely Christian theological concept and practice. Later in this chapter, I will discuss the need to evangelize as a component of various approaches that will assist in mitigating racism.

To further highlight the distinctive nature of grace in Christianity, Dr. Charlie Bing wrote in his book, "Simply by Grace," the following:

> A question posed years ago at a British conference on world religions sparked a lively debate: What makes Christianity unique among all the other religions in this world? Some argued that it was the Incarnation, others, the Resurrection. But some replied that other religions had similar beliefs. When C.S. Lewis walked into the room, someone explained their quandary. 'Oh, that's easy,' he said, 'It's grace.' How does Christianity distinguish itself from every other religion? Simply by grace."

Dr. Bing went on to elaborate, "that's how you become a Christian, be eternally saved, know you are eternally saved, live the Christian life, and that's motivation behind serving God and others . . . simply by grace.[2]

To accentuate Dr. Bing's point, here is a Scripture on grace found in the Book of Ephesians, "For by grace you have been saved through faith, and that not of yourselves; *it is* the gift of God, not of works, lest anyone should boast. For we are His workmanship, created in Christ Jesus for good works, which God prepared beforehand that we should walk in them." This Scripture delineates the truth that we are saved by God's charis, received through faith, and are saved for the purpose of performing good works as God has designed.

Because the apostle Paul inserted the term grace in the Book of Romans about 28 different times, it is wise to highlight at least one of those Scriptures found in that treatise: "for all have sinned and fall short of the glory of God, being justified freely by His *grace* through the redemption that is in Christ Jesus, whom God set forth *as* a propitiation by His blood, through faith, to demonstrate His righteousness, because in His forbearance God had passed over the sins that were previously committed, to demonstrate at the present time His righteousness, that He might be just and the justifier of the one who has faith in Jesus." (Rom 3:23-26, emphasis added) This Scripture informs the believer that those who trust Christ as Savior are justified (or acquitted from the guilty charge of sin) freely by God's grace, redeemed in Christ (purchased with the blood of Jesus Christ), declared righteous (a legal term of art denoting justification), and received through faith. Further, the Baker Encyclopedia explains it as follows,

> God's grace manifested in Jesus Christ makes it possible for God to forgive sinners and to gather them in the church, the new covenant community. During his ministry, Jesus repeatedly pronounced the words of forgiveness on a great number of sinners and ministered God's benevolent succor to a variety of desperate human needs.[3]

As a communicable attribute of God, He has not only allowed His children to demonstrate grace in their relationships with both believers and unbelievers but also encourages it. Gilbert Bilezikian makes the following proposition,

> Finally, God's grace manifested in Jesus Christ makes it possible for God to cause believers to reflect his grace in their character and relationships. The irreducible condition for receiving God's grace is humility (Jas 4:6; 1 Pet 5:5). Such humility in relation to God enables believers to practice humility in regard to other people. From a position of grace, they can set aside selfishness and conceit in order to treat others with deference (Phil 2:3, 4) in an attitude of mutual servanthood (Eph 5:21), and in a spirit of mutual forgiveness (Mt 18:23–35) so that even their communication can exhibit divine grace (Col 4:6). Since the grace of Jesus Christ constitutes the existential context of the lives and relationships of believers, they are exhorted not to pervert the grace of God into ungodly practice (Jude 4) but instead to grow in the grace of the Lord (2 Pet 3:18).[4]

When we think of grace extended among humanity, the name Anthony Ray Hinton comes to mind. Mr. Hinton, a Black man, was born in 1956 in the state of Alabama and was wrongly charged for killing two restaurant managers in Birmingham, Alabama during 1985. Mr. Hinton faced an all-White jury who had no DNA evidence, no eyewitnesses, and ignored a rock-solid alibi given by Hinton's employer. Just to offer more insight into the sign of the times, the arresting officer told Mr. Hinton that he didn't care whether or not Hinton had committed the crimes but expected Hinton to be convicted because he would face White police officers, a White district attorney, a White judge, and an all-White jury in the Alabama court system! Unfortunately, and without prophetic inspiration, the officer was correct. Mr. Hinton was convicted of killing the two restaurant managers in Birmingham, Alabama. This conviction was upheld to the Alabama State Supreme Court. Subsequently, the State placed him in solitary confinement and on death row where he was incarcerated for 28 years. During that time, he witnessed 54 men walk past his cell to their electric chair destiny. In fact, Mr. Hinton explained that he could smell the burning of human flesh, as his cell was situated in close proximity to the capital punishment chair.

However, as God would have it, during those 28 years, one of the 54 men that Mr. Hinton encountered on death row was one Mr. Henry Francis Hays. Mr. Hays was a self-proclaimed White supremacist and KKK member. Mr. Hays was on death row for lynching Michael Donald, a 19-year-old Black man. Notwithstanding Mr. Hays' hatred towards Blacks, Mr. Hinton decided to extend grace to Mr. Hays. To that end, Mr. Hinton taught Mr. Hays how to read and helped Mr. Hays overcome some of his racist proclivities towards Blacks. Because of grace, these two unlikely individuals (Hinton and Hays) in Alabama and on death row created a strong bond up to the very day in which Mr. Hays was executed. This is the power of God's grace and just how effective it can be! Grace can obliterate the racial divide and can bring together (in a wholesome and kind relationship) the most improbable candidates.

For a happy ending to a most unpleasant story, Bryan Stevenson of the Equal Justice Initiative (a non-profit law firm based in Montgomery, Alabama) extended grace and represented Mr. Hinton in court. As a result, Mr. Hinton's conviction was overturned by the United States Supreme Court in 2015. Later, the district attorney of Jefferson County dropped all charges against Mr. Hinton, whereupon he became a free man once again.

While God does not coerce Christians into practicing grace, He has certainly prepared the way for those who possess the desire to do so (like Mr. Hinton). We also see this practice of grace promoted by Jesus in the parable concerning the "Good Samaritan" found in Luke 10. When Jesus taught this parable, He did not indicate the ethnicity of the man who encountered thieves during his travels from Jerusalem to Jericho. However, the hearers of this parable probably assumed that the man was Jewish based on Jesus' audience and the itinerary of the man in the parable. So, for the sake of this discussion, we will identify the man as Jewish. Moreover, this man was robbed, wounded, and left for dead by these thieves. Note, the priest and the Levite (both Jewish) saw the man dying but did not approach him and render the needed aid. However, it was a Samaritan man that came to assist this Jewish man. While the Samaritan was the least likely to render assistance, he had compassion, bandaged the wounds, reserved a room at an inn for the injured man, and paid the innkeeper to care for the man until his return. Of course, this was a powerful act of grace because there was great enmity between Jews and Samaritans dating back to when the Nation of Israel divided, with 10 tribes relocating in the north and 2 tribes remaining in the south. This hatred continued as witnessed by Jesus' encounter with the woman at the well in John 4. The woman said, "How is it that You, being a Jew, ask a drink from me, a Samaritan woman?" For Jews have no dealings with Samaritans. Therefore, with respect to the Samaritan in the parable, He exercised great grace that superseded racism, prejudices, bigotry, and the like which existed during those ancient times. Continuing Jesus' point of the parable, we must extend grace to everyone that needs it, and we all need it. In short, grace can and should play a vital role in the battle to mitigate and (wherever possible) defeat racism, which brings us to our next significant word, racism.

So, what is racism? Here are a few definitions to ponder, "*The belief that some races are inherently superior (physically, intellectually, or culturally) to others and therefore have a right to dominate them;*"[5] "*Racism—is the abuse of power by a "racial" group that is more powerful than one or more other groups in order to exclude, demean, damage, control, or destroy the less powerful groups. Racism confers benefits upon the dominant group that includes psychological feelings of superiority, social privilege, economic-position, or political power;"*[6] and *"Theologically understood, racism is a vaulting, arrogant human attempt to seize for itself that special status which in Biblical thought is called election. As such racism is a profound perversion of election, for in Biblical definition election belongs to God alone, the God who exalts the humble and casts down the proud."*[7]

When discussing the concept of racism, Jemar Tisby in his book *The Color of Compromise* writes the following, "What do we mean when we talk about racism? Beverly Daniel Tatum provides a shorthand definition: racism is a system of oppression based on race. Notice Tatum's emphasis on systemic oppression. Racism can operate through impersonal systems and not simply through the malicious words and actions of individuals. Another definition explains racism as prejudice plus power."[8]

In the book entitled *Divided by Faith*, authors Michael O. Emerson and Christian Smith point out the misconceptions some people hold concerning racism. For instance, they identify the following misguided view, "Racism is viewed as an irrational psychological phenomenon that is the product of individuals, and is evidenced in overt, usually hostile behavior. It is the driving force behind anything negative about race relations."[9] I agree with Emerson and Smith because this understanding of racism fails to acknowledge that groups and institutions can be and usually are a source of racism and that the practice of racism is not always overt. The two authors go on to proffer the following approach to racism,

> The framework we here use—racialization—reflects that adaptation. It understands that racial practices that reproduce racial division in the contemporary United States '(1) are increasingly covert, (2) are embedded in normal operations of institutions, (3) avoid direct racial terminology, and individual, overt prejudice or the free-floating irrational driver of race problems, but the collective misuse of power that results in diminished life opportunities for some racial groups. Racism is a changing ideology with the constant and rational purpose

of perpetuating and justifying a social system that is racialized. The justification may include individual, overt prejudice, and discrimination, but these are not necessary.[10]

Here, by definition, one must take notice that racism affords the misuse and/or abuse of power by one group over another. Of course, the one exercising or enjoying the benefits derived from such abuse or misuse is a racist.

Racism has existed since time immemorial and is demonstrated by Pharaoh when he placed the Israelites in four hundred years of Egyptian bondage in Ex 1:8–11, "Now there arose a new king over Egypt, who did not know Joseph. And he said to his people, "Look, the people of the children of Israel *are* more and mightier than we; come, let us deal shrewdly with them, lest they multiply, and it happen, in the event of war, that they also join our enemies and fight against us, and *so* go up out of the land." Therefore they set taskmasters over them to afflict them with their burdens. And they built for Pharaoh supply cities, Pithom and Raamses." Pharaoh's racist approach to Israel was derived from ignorance (he did not know Egypt's history with Joseph) and fear (Israel was greater in number than the Egyptians and they might join enemy armies). The latter reasoning seemed to be based on the possibility of what could or might happen as opposed to Egypt's actual historical experience with Israel. Such sentiment is the typical underpinnings of racism. That is, many racist practices are born out of fear and ignorance.

To summarize the key elements, the definition of racism informs the reader that the abuse and misuse of power are in operation to harm one group for the benefit of another, it creates an "us" versus "them" mentality, a pseudo-caste system, a display of pride and arrogance, and a sense of superiority and inferiority (of course, depending on your vantage point). Additionally, it may surface by omission or commission and can be overt as well as covert. Lastly, racism permeates and manifests itself in the individual, in cultural mores, in institutions (even our churches), and in the society of the powerful majority group. No doubt, racism is ubiquitous, and if people are not careful and vigilant, every member of society will be imprisoned by it, without regard to ethnicity! To be clear, I believe the Bible teaches that there is only one race but multiple ethnicities. This matter is further explained later in this chapter.

Joseph Brandt explains racism in the following manner, "As this book progresses it should become clear that racism affects nearly every aspect of our lives. Wherever one goes, whatever stone is overturned in the field of social turmoil, whatever the issue, one encounters the persistent, ever-present problem of racism. An understanding of racism is needed, therefore, not only by those who are directly involved in issues of racial justice, but also by those who work with all the other issues of justice and social change."[11] To summarize, racism is pervasive and can permeate all aspects of society.

The next key term in our discussion is the word, prejudice. This term denotes the idea of racism without the power component. It is to judge others or deploy broad generalizations based on external factors and preconceived notions before any real evidence is known about an individual or group. It is in essence judging someone based on information derived from ignorance or a flawed/misguided database while exhibiting partiality to one over another. Brandt states, "Everyone is prejudiced, but not everyone is racist. To be prejudiced means to have opinions without knowing the facts and to hold onto those opinions, even after contrary facts are known. To be racially prejudiced means to have distorted opinions about people of other races."[12]

James, the half-brother of our Lord Jesus Christ, (Matt 13:55; Gal 1:19) reminded the diaspora concerning prejudice in the epistle he wrote, "My brethren, do not hold the faith of our Lord Jesus Christ, *the Lord* of glory, with partiality. For if there should come into your assembly a man with gold rings, in fine apparel, and there should also come in a poor man in filthy clothes, and you pay attention to the one wearing the fine clothes and say to him, "You sit here in a good place," and say to the poor man, "You stand there," or, "Sit here at my footstool," have you not shown partiality among yourselves, and become judges with evil thoughts?" (Jas 2:1–4) It should be noted that James was speaking to believers (my brethren) who were prejudging people on the basis of external factors (looking rich as opposed to looking poor). James pointed out that such an attitude and behavior are inconsistent with faith in Jesus Christ (see also Jas 2:5–7; Matt 22:16; Acts 10:34; Gal 2:6). They cause division within the assembly and expose one's evil thoughts. Later, James wrote, "Therefore, to him who knows to do good and does not do *it,* to him it is sin." In other words, if you know what is the right thing to do and don't do it, you have committed sin (see Jas 4:17).

The next term requiring scrutiny is bigotry. Bigotry promotes the denotation of intolerance. Merriam Webster defines bigotry as, "obstinate or intolerant devotion to one's own opinions and prejudices."[13] Baird and Rosenbaum offer the following observation, "When we harbor negative passions 'impersonally' against groups rather than against individuals who have deliberately or inadvertently offended us, then we are prone to intolerance and hate. We become sources of bigotry and prejudice, and we are liable to abuse or injure others not because of anything they have done but merely because they have some characteristic—race or gender or nationality or sexuality— beyond their own choosing."[14] Bigotry seems to be a close cousin to prejudice and hatred, as the three are interconnected. As the other terms examined, one can discover bigotry in the Bible. One writer stated the following,

> Paul was stressing that nothing—race, education, income, social status, language, political differences—was to provide the platform from which bigotry separated God's people. Let's take a look at one more verse in this blog to drive the point home and hopefully make it more personal. There was a prayer famous in the time of Jesus and the Apostle Paul in which men would pray to God thanking Him for not making them a Gentile, a slave or a woman. So in his writing to the churches in the region of Galatia, Paul explicitly addresses the issue by saying the following.
>
> There is neither Jew nor Greek, there is neither slave nor free, there is no male and female, for you are all one in Christ Jesus. Galatians 3:28. [ESV] Paul was saying to those who had prayed or heard that prayer that those statements are coming from a bigoted perspective and have been overturned for those who accept Christ.[15]

Therefore, bigotry is an intolerance that is enveloped in both hatred and prejudice.

Another term of art in this arena of ethnic relations is discrimination, and it is the concomitant action to racism, prejudice, and the like. In other words, it places one's racist and prejudicial principles into practice. In his book White Fragility, Robin DiAngelo states, "Discrimination is action based on prejudice. These actions include ignoring, exclusion, threats, ridicule, slander, and violence. For example, if hatred is the emotion we feel because of our prejudice, extreme acts of discrimination, such as violence, may follow. These forms of discrimination are generally clear and recognizable. But if what we feel is more subtle, such as mild discomfort, the discrimination is likely to also be subtle, even hard to detect."[16]

As people look through the lens of prejudice, hatred, and racism, people are destined to manifest these negative attributes through their behaviors. The ungracious and sinful practices are generated in the head, make their way to the heart, and ultimately are exhibited in one's daily habits.

An example of discrimination is found in Gal 2, where Paul confronted the false brethren as well as Peter for discriminating against Titus specifically and the Gentiles in general. There, Paul articulated that Gentile believers were not required to undergo circumcision to be saved and that Peter was a hypocrite for not eating with the Gentiles when certain men arrived in Antioch from Jerusalem. Therefore, Paul confronted racism and prejudice (powerful Jews prejudging Gentiles) and discrimination (Peter ceased eating with the Gentiles).

This chapter now turns its gaze on identifying various manifestations of racism and its ubiquitous nature. Firstly, let me confess that I do not know of any black person over twenty-one that has not experienced some form of racism (including its protégés . . . prejudice, bigotry, discrimination, and white privilege). When I say, "some form," I mean:

- The police officers who pull you over when you are driving because you "look suspicious" or that you are driving a car that is "too nice" for you (must be a drug dealer). This is called "driving while black" or profiling.

- You are beaten, choked, shot, and killed, while violent white offenders are taken into custody without incident.

- People follow you around in stores because they think you are going to steal simply because you are a person of color.

- The employment practices that are designed to have you the last one hired but the first one fired (if you are even fortunate to get hired); or based on your name, they attempt to determine your ethnicity and eliminate your resume as a candidate for the corporate or ministry position before the interviewing committee reviews it.

- The teacher that you admired and looked up to tells you that you will never amount to anything.

- The colleague who tells you, "You are not like the rest of them."

- The people who do not believe you live in this luxury apartment or work at this facility. So, you must produce credentials validating who you are and your right to exist there (when others are not required to do the same).

- The legislature that "redlines" your neighborhood, which destines you to a separate but unequal education.

- The bank that will not extend you a loan based on your zip code.

- There were times when the National Football League (NFL) thought that a black person was not intelligent enough to become a quarterback. Now, there are approximately 9 starting quarterbacks in the NFL.

I could go on and on, but time nor space will permit! Obviously, this list is not meant to fully address every situation, but it is illustrative of the many insults that black people and other people of color are confronted with each day. Insults that others rarely, if ever, encounter. Worse yet, these unfortunate encounters are seen affecting multiple generations in families. This short list of examples is not the so-called "generational curse" that folks espouse. This is (in most, if not all cases) a result of systemic racism.

Secondly, what can we do as believers to frustrate racism, prejudice, bigotry, discrimination, and the like? To mitigate racism and its protégés, believers must recognize where it exists, evangelize others, possess a biblical view of race, promote love, and practice grace wherever and whenever possible in place of racism, and pray.

If we are to forge ahead in our progressive sanctification and in our effort to please God during our spiritual walk with Him, we must recognize the reality of racism and where it exists. That is, these dastardly concepts and practices do exist in America and around the world. It is a part of Satan's evil and counterfeit plan to prevent believers from becoming and accomplishing all that God wants His believers to achieve and undertake for the kingdom of God. In addition, the issue is not whether it exists, but where to unearth it. Thus, it is difficult to ferret out racism if you do not know where to search for it so that you can offer grace in its place, which is one of the objectives of this chapter.

Consequently, believers must realize that they have been impacted by it either due to the benefits derived from society's system of racism and the like, or as the unfortunate de facto target of it. One of our great challenges is that these concepts are woven into the fabric of our society, at all levels, in a variety of entities and institutions, and people. This makes such an evil and formidable foe as there is no one place or person to blame because it is so ubiquitous.

Nonetheless, believers must acknowledge that racism and the like emanate from a sinful heart and as long as sin exists, so too will racism. As stated previously, however, we can mitigate but not eradicate racism, and churches as well as individual believers must assume a key role in achieving such a biblical cause.

Evangelism is a crucial initiative in mitigating racism. Remember, racism is a sin. Therefore, the strategy for effectively combatting racism is to evangelize and introduce unbelievers to Jesus Christ. So that no one is deluded, Christians practice racism too (because believers sin), which means that evangelism alone is not the panacea to curing all societal ills generated by racism. However, Christianity can and should play a vital role in combatting racism.

In the introductory remarks of this chapter, I wrote about my Dad and that he trusted Christ as his Savior at an early age. God regenerated his heart, and as a result, his change of heart afforded him a transformed view of people and his difficult circumstance while living in the Jim Crow South. Also, his thought process and behavior positively affected others who were around him. Thus, believers must evangelize so that others might exemplify the attitudes and actions of Jesus Christ and not engage in racism.

In Acts 1:8, Luke the physician pinned these words of our Lord Jesus Christ, "But you shall receive power when the Holy Spirit has come upon you; and you shall be witnesses to Me in Jerusalem, and in all Judea and Samaria, and to the end of the earth.'" This verse outlines the entire Book of Acts, and it addresses the power of the Holy Spirit (the power behind birthing and propagating the church movement), the person of Christ (the Lord who commissions), and the program of Christ (worldwide witnessing for Him). In chapters 1–12, Peter is the primary spokesperson, evangelizing Jews and Samaritans (a mixed ethnicity of Jews and Assyrians). To complete the outline of the book, the apostle Paul assumed the role of the central evangelist who proclaimed the gospel message to the Gentiles in chapters 13–28.

Initially, Jesus sent His disciples into the world (to follow His designated travel itinerary) with the purpose of evangelizing and winning souls for the kingdom of God. At that time, the end of the earth was probably Rome. Nevertheless, as a matter of application, we too possess the responsibility and commission to convey our witness for Christ to the ends of the earth, wherever that might take us.

As noted above, believers must play a leading role in this arena if a significant impact on racism will ever occur. Dr. Tony Evans agrees with this view as he stated in his book *Oneness Embraced*,

> It is my contention that the fundamental cause of racial problems in America lies squarely with the church's failure to come to grips with this issue from a biblical perspective. The truth that has been missed is that God does much of what He does predicated on what His church is or is not doing (Ephesians 3:10). In the same way that God's purpose, presence, and power in the Old Testament was to flow from His people and through the temple into the world (Ezekiel 47:1–12), even so today it should flow from the church into the broader society. When the church fails

to act in concert with God's prescribed agenda, then God often chooses to postpone His active involvement until His people are prepared to respond. Our failure to respond to this issue of biblical oneness has allowed what never should have been a problem in the first place to continue for hundreds of years.[17]

Evans has articulated his point of view quite well, and it would behoove other church leaders (clergy and laity alike) to join him in advancing the same or similar tactics against this plague on the society in which the church exists.

Therefore, to diminish the impact of racism, it is crucial that the church is actively involved and is central to this approach. As stated previously, racism is a sin that is derived from a sinful heart (see Jer 17:9), and the church is divinely and uniquely positioned to combat it with the message of salvation (justification, sanctification, and glorification) that engenders a regenerated heart by God's grace through faith. The apostle Paul reminded us in 2 Cor 5:17 that God can bring about a situation where a person (new creation) can and should manifest an outward change in himself once he trusts Christ as Savior. This text states, "Therefore, if anyone *is* in Christ, *he is* a new creation; old things have passed away; behold, all things have become new." The Greek phrase new-creation (kainé ktisis) carries the sense that the old-self has passed away and is replaced by the born-again-self that has become new in Christ. (See also Col 3:5-11.) This does not mean that our sinful nature no longer exists. On the other hand, it does mean that our sin nature no longer has rule over us (see Rom 6). That is, believers must learn to yield to the Holy Spirit and not to their sin nature. Additionally, a significant transformation takes place that includes the indwelling of the Holy Spirit (Rom 8:9), the forgiveness of sin (Eph 1:7; Col 3:13; 4:32; Heb 8:12; 10:17–18; 1 John 1:9), and the imputed righteousness of Christ Jesus (2 Cor 5:21), just to name a few. Lewis Sperry Chafer (founder of Dallas Theological Seminary) identified 34 different blessings that are bestowed upon a person the moment he believes in Christ as Savior. Later in this same pericope (2 Cor 5) at verse 20, Paul explained that believers are ambassadors for Christ, and as Christ's representatives, we evangelize with the message of reconciliation. Believers are called upon to make an appeal to and urge unbelievers to trust Christ as Savior, which in turn could and should have a substantial influence on mitigating racism.

Not that believers need to be incentivized to evangelize others, nonetheless, God has promised and set aside rewards at the Judgment Seat of Christ (1 Cor 3:12–15; 2 Cor 5:10–11; Rom 14:10–12) for those who evangelize. See 1 Thess 2:19, where the apostle Paul reminded believers that God will distribute crowns of rejoicing for evangelism. Also, Dan 12:3 states, "Those who are wise shall shine like the brightness of the firmament, and those who turn many to righteousness like the stars forever and ever."

Another reason for the church to engage in thwarting racism is the Great Commission to make disciples for Christ. Once a person is successfully evangelized, members of the body of Christ should facilitate the new believer's participation in a discipleship program. Jesus commanded us in Matt 28:19-20, "'Go therefore and make disciples of all the nations, baptizing them in the name of the Father and of the Son and of the Holy Spirit, teaching them to observe all things that I have commanded you; and lo, I am with you always, *even* to the end of the age.' Amen." As one of my colleagues would say, the discipleship plan should incorporate components that are relational, intentional, progressive, and experiential (R-I-P-E-). All of which must include helping people eschew racist attitudes and discriminatory practices and tender grace instead. Jesus' command included all nations (various ethnicities) as our target population to disciple, without exemptions. (Also, see Mark 11:15-17 where Jesus stated that God's house is a place for all nations.) This means to disciple people that do not look like you as well! Here, the words from James, the half-brother of Jesus comes to mind, "Therefore, to him who knows to do good and does not do *it*, to him it is sin." In other words, Jesus' commission calls upon believers to pursue all people for discipleship regardless of ethnicity, and to willfully not do it is sin.

What does it mean to be a disciple of Jesus Christ? According to Dr. David R. Anderson, "*A disciple is one who is fully devoted to following Jesus Christ. To be fully devoted to following Christ means, you must be willing to give up and/or say goodbye to everything up to and including your life.*" A person is deemed "willing" when he is ready, eager, and/or prepared to do what God calls him to do, which also includes avoiding the practice of racism, prejudice, discrimination as well as combatting them too. In Rom 12:1, the apostle Paul encouraged us to become a "living sacrifice" for the cause of Christ (fully committed). (See also Matt 16:24-27; Luke 14:25-35; Gal 2:20.) To sacrifice can sometimes mean relinquishing old beliefs and behaviors and replacing them with the attitudes and actions of Jesus Christ.

It is imperative that church leadership involve themselves in addressing the racism problem as mentioned above, and Emerson and Smith proffered the following statement, "Religion has tremendous potential for mitigating racial division and inequality. Most religions teach love, respect, and equality of all peoples. They often teach of the errors inherent in racial prejudice and discrimination. They frequently proclaim the need to embrace all people. They speak of the need for fairness and justice. They often teach that selfishness and acting in self-interested ways are counter to the will of the divine."[18]

In an effort to diminish racism, believers must possess and help others to embrace a biblical view concerning race. That is, from God's perspective, He created one race of people, the human race. During the antediluvian period, God created Adam and Eve and called them to procreate, which they did. In delineating Adam's lineage, Moses (the author of Genesis) wrote about a descendant whose name was Lamech. Now, based on Gen 5:28, Lamech had a son named Noah. During Gen 6-9, Noah became the prominent character dealing with God, and God destroyed the world by flood but spared Noah, his wife, his three sons (Shem, Ham, and Japheth), the three wives of the sons, and animal life. Moreover, in Gen 10 (which displays the table of nations), Noah's sons repopulated the entire world based on God's directive (see Gen 9:1). Thus, Gen 10:32 states, "These *were* the families of the sons of Noah, according to their generations, in their nations; and from these the nations were divided on the earth after the flood." Note that God created one race of people, via one family (mishpachah is the Hebrew word for clan or extended family), into one nation (goy is the Hebrew word for nations or people), with multiple generations (tôledôt is a Hebrew word that is translated generations here), and directed them to scatter throughout the earth. In summary, God created "one" big family, and we are all relatives. This biblical truth is not designed to obfuscate or obliterate our diverse characteristics, as God intended for them to subsist. However, it should be a moment of celebrating God's workmanship, who He created to be unified and to do perform good works (see Eph 2:10).

This exact concept of "oneness" is intended for the body of Christ also. For example, Gal 3:28 states, "There is neither Jew nor Greek, there is neither slave nor free, there is neither male nor female; for you are all one in Christ Jesus." Additionally, the apostle Paul wrote this oneness concept in Eph 2:14-16.

The next focus of the fight against racism is love. It is yet another weapon in the war against racism. That is, God's love (agape) is the love we should promote. Dr. Anderson defines this love as unending, undeserved, unlimited, unselfish, and unconditional (see Rom 5:5-11; 1 Cor 13:1-8). By its very definition, love is other-centered and seeks the finest good for someone else. This is the type of love that you cannot earn, and you cannot lose. When we engage in loving others in this fashion, we behave in a manner consistent with God's commands. (See the Great Command at Matt 22:37-40.) Also, love is the antidote for racism because you can't exercise a racist attitude or some type of bigotry if you are focused on obtaining the "finest or highest" good for others (including people that don't look like you). Remember, one of the hallmarks of a believer is that we love one another (John 13:34-35; 1 John 2:9-11; 3:9-11; 4:7–14). Jesus has made this truth clear for believers to grasp on multiple occasions.

Next, we are encouraged to practice grace. This means that believers must learn to share the grace message with others as often as God presents the opportunity for us to do so and practice it too. So, what does the practice of grace look like in our pugilistic efforts to stem the tide of racism? This means believers must act, and not passively stand by or sit and watch racism permeate our homes, our cities, our churches, our government, our country, and for that matter, our world. In thinking about this subject, I was reminded of just how much I learn from my children. Here recently, Mark II (my son) explained to me the difference between not being a racist and becoming an "anti-racist." While both categories of people do not embrace racism, the key distinction, he explained, is that the "anti-racist" has a duty to act; a duty to volitionally and assertively stop racist behavior in his/her presence or where it exists. Let me further articulate what this means: (1) Don't embrace implicit biases and stereotypes, but rather challenge those stereotypes and speak out against them: for example, all Blacks are lazy, Hispanics are only worthy enough to mow your lawn, all Native Americans are drunken liars; (2) If you hear a racial epithet of any kind in your presence, do not be afraid to confront the speaker, shut him or her down, and speak the truth in love; (3) If you hear insulting ethnic jokes, state your displeasure, and if possible, shut them down; (4) If you see a person of color alone in a room full of white people all talking to one another and not that individual, go initiate a conversation with that person of color carefully but authentically. I cannot tell you how many times I have seen this happen. However, one time I witnessed just the opposite. One of our board of trustee members at Grace School of Theology left his comfortable circle of friends to engage two African Americans who were clearly alone in a sea of white people. Each time I see this board member, it brings back fond memories of his expression of love and his anti-racist proclivity; and (5) Don't be like the three officers that failed to stop Officer Chauvin in the killing of Mr. George Floyd. Instead, ACT! Sadly, both Mr. Chauvin's actions and the other three officers' inaction resulted in tragedy. Please don't let that be your testimony . . . that is, your actions or inaction result in someone's heartbreaking experience.

Lastly, I learned from my Dad at a young age the importance of prayer. One of our greatest weapons to combat racism, sin, and wickedness is prayer. Remember, Jesus taught us to always pray (Luke 18:1), the apostle Paul said to pray without ceasing (1 Thess 5:17), and James said the effectual fervent prayers of the righteous avails much (Jas 5:16). So, what do you pray for? Pray for the healing of our nation and the world. Pray for reforms at every level of our society starting with the hearts of humanity, with city, state, and federal officials so that policies, practices, and procedures are divested of racist agendas and tendencies. Pray for justice and equal protection under the law for everyone. And pray that God grants you the courage and wisdom to reject racism, prejudice, bigotry, discrimination and the like, and replace them with grace and anti-racist ethics.

If grace is to have a positive impact on race relations, believers must understand key terms related to grace and racism, know where to discover racism because of its ubiquitous nature, as well as explore biblical approaches to sharing grace. Moreover, believers should learn to appreciate that racism is a sin that is antithetical to God's desires for His people. Also, as long as sin exists, racism will live on as well. Moreover, we can mitigate but not eradicate racism.

In short, humanity's greatest hope and expectations lie with the church advancing the war against racism and the like because we offer the free grace message of salvation in Jesus Christ, our Lord. It is Him and Him alone who can change the hearts and minds of people. This fact is observed in Prov 21:1, "The king's heart *is* in the hand of the Lord, *Like* the rivers of water; He turns it wherever He wishes."

May each believer become a party of one and share the grace of our Lord Jesus Christ with others (even people that do not look like us).

---

[1] William Arndt et al., *A Greek-English Lexicon of the New Testament and Other Early Christian Literature* (Chicago: University of Chicago Press, 2000), 1079–1080.

[2] Charles C. Bing, *Simply by Grace: An Introduction to God's Life-Changing Gift* (Kregel Publications, 2009), 11.

[3] Gilbert Bilezikian, "Grace," *Baker Encyclopedia of the Bible* (Grand Rapids, MI: Baker Book House, 1988), 899.

[4] Ibid., 900.

[5] *The American Heritage® New Dictionary of Cultural Literacy*, 3rd ed. Copyright © 2005 by Houghton Mifflin Company.

[6] Susan E. Davies and Sister Paul Teresa Hennessee, eds., *Ending Racism In The Church* (Cleveland, Ohio: The Pilgrim Press, 1998),1.

[7] Carl F. H Henry, ed., *Bakers Dictionary of Christian Ethics*, excerpt from an article on racism by James Daane, 564.

[8] Jemar Tisby, *The Color of Compromise* (Zondervan, 2020), 16, Kindle Edition.

[9] Michael O. Emerson and Christian Smith, *Divided by Faith, Evangelical Religion and the Problem of Race in America* (New York, New York: Oxford University Press, 2000), 8.

[10] Ibid., p. 9.

[11] Joseph Barndt, *Dismantling Racism*, 113-115, Kindle Edition.

[12] Ibid., 359-361.

[13] "bigotry," *Merriam Webster Dictionary*, https://www.merriam-webster.com/dictionary/bigotry, accessed October 25, 2020.

[14] Robert M. Baird and Stuart E. Rosenbaum, *Hatred, Bigotry, and Prejudice - Definitions, Causes & Solutions (Contemporary Issues)*, 64-66, Kindle Edition.

[15] "What the Bible Has to Say About Bigotry," October 15, 2019, https://www.fcc-m.com/post/what-the-bible-has-to-say-about-bigotry, accessed October 25, 2020.

[16] Robin J. DiAngelo, *White Fragility: Why It's So Hard for White People to Talk About Racism* (Beacon Press, 2018), 20, Kindle Edition.

[17] Tony Evans, *Oneness Embraced: Reconciliation, the Kingdom, and How We Are Stronger Together* (Moody Publishers, 2015), 18, Kindle Edition, 18.

[18] Michael O. Emerson and Christian Smith, *Divided by Faith, Evangelical Religion and the Problem of Race in America*, 153.

Conclusion

Dr. Fred Chay

The core of all theological thought and the center that holds all Biblical truth together is the Glorious Grace of God! As Lewis Sperry Chafer said, "Pure grace is neither treating a person as he deserves, nor treating a person better than he deserves, but treating a person without the slightest reference to what he deserves." We have tried to reveal how the grace of God in the lives of His people can manifest itself in family, vocation, and ministry.

The Grace of God toward us is unearned and therefore should be unrestricted from us to others. When we find it difficult to extend grace to others, it is often because we have lost focus on God's grace to ourselves.

- Romans 3:24—Being justified freely by His **grace** through the redemption that is in Christ Jesus.

- Romans 5:2—Through whom also we have access by faith into this **grace** in which we stand and rejoice in hope of the glory of God.

- Ephesians 1:6—To the praise of the glory of His **grace**, by which He has made us accepted in the Beloved.

- Ephesians 1:7—In Him we have redemption through His blood, the forgiveness of sins, <u>according to the riches of</u> His **grace**.

- Ephesians 2:5—Even when we were dead in our trespasses, He <u>made us alive together with Christ</u> (by **grace** you have been saved).

Culture can be challenging to navigate and negotiate. People can be confounding with all of their uniqueness. Life can be confusing. But in all of its confrontations and considerations, grace is the cure to living in a lost and dying world, and in living with each other.

The Grace of God has been granted from the garden of Eden to the garden of Gethsemane, and to all of us. It's only natural then that we live by grace.